P9-DMC-332

CAPTAINS
OF
CONSCIOUSNESS

OUACHITA TECHNICAL COLLEGE

CAPTAINS OF CONSCIOUSNESS

Advertising and the Social Roots
of the Consumer Culture
by
Stuart Ewen

McGraw-Hill Book Company

New York / St. Louis / San Francisco
Toronto / Mexico / Düsseldorf

OUACHITA TECHNICAL COLLEGE

Book design by Andrew Roberts.

Copyright © 1976 by Stuart Ewen.

All rights reserved.
Printed in the United States of America.
No part of this publication may be reproduced,
stored in a retrieval system, or transmitted, in any form
or by any means, electronic, mechanical, photocopying, recording,
or otherwise, without the prior written permission of the
publisher.

7 8 9 FGRFGR   8 3 2
First McGraw-Hill Paperback Edition, 1977

Library of Congress Cataloging in Publication Data
Ewen, Stuart.
    Captains of consciousness.

    Bibliography: p.
    Includes index.
    1.   Advertising—Social aspects—United States.
  2.   Industry—Social aspects—United States.
  3.   Consumers—United States. I. Title.
HF5813.U6E94   659.1'0973   75-34432
   ISBN 0-07-019846-2

Copyright, 1926, by Horace Liveright; copyright, 1954, by E. E.
Cummings. Reprinted from *Complete Poems 1913–1962* by E. E.
Cummings by permission of Harcourt Brace Jovanovich, Inc.

HF
5813
.U6
E94
1976

For Liz, Paul
and Sam

ACKNOWLEDGMENTS

Work on this book began in 1969. Since that time, a number of people have been extremely helpful and comforting. I would like to thank and make mention of those whose friendship and support have contributed to the strengths of the study and analysis.

Much of the research entailed was completed at the library of the University of Rochester and at the Widener Library and Baker Business Library at Harvard University. I have also received a good deal of help from my friends in the Marxist Institute for a New History (MINH); their aid and advice has been invaluable.

People who read the manuscript in part or as a whole, and who made suggestions for improvement, include Linda Gordon, Russell Jacoby, Gail Pellett, Bernard Flynn, John Strawn, David Nasaw, Andrew

Ewen, Wini Breines, Naomi Glauberman, Phyllis Ewen, Dan Raskin, Ann Weissman, Richard Elman, Danny Schechter, George Rawick, Jeff Herf, Joel Kovel, Carol Lopate, Berenice Hoffman, and my agent, Gerard McCauley. Stanley Aronowitz, Ros Baxandall, Paul Breines and Loren Baritz all made immeasurable contributions in their reading and support of my work. My parents, Sol and Sylvia Ewen, and also Roger and Frances Wunderlich, have been supportive of my work.

Margaret Cerullo worked closely with me in preparing the manuscript, making many valuable editorial suggestions along the way. My editor at McGraw-Hill, Joyce Johnson, has been an understanding and helpful champion of this book, wonderful to work with, as was Veronica Windholz, who aided in turning this into a book.

Most of all, I wish to thank Elizabeth Ewen. A constant friend and person with whom I could discuss materials and ideas, she is, in many ways, my co-conspirator in this book's realization.

CONTENTS

Preface:
The Social Crisis
of Industrialization

Mass reproduction is aided especially by the reproduction of masses. . . .

—WALTER BENJAMIN, "The Work of Art
in the Age of Mechanical Reproduction"

This is a study of the emergence of important aspects of American industrial culture in the twentieth century: mass consumption and modern advertising. The growth of these phenomena reaches to the root of what is commonly described as "mass culture," the flowering of which has been no less significant to the American landscape than the first appearance of factories in meadows in the 1830s and '40s. From a present-day vantage point, it is impossible to separate the emergence of mass culture from the industrial context. Yet little has been done to locate the development of this culture within the context of industrial history, particularly within the context of the *social* history of American industrialization.

Mass culture, like industrialization itself, has too often been viewed as a self-generating process, its history depicted like a "clock without a spring," the social energies in its development ignored. Although people have been well aware of the ways in which industrial capitalism has actively permeated our environment, such perceptions have been characterized and mystified by ideas of *progress* and *development* measured by changes in *the machine.* The social reality of this penetration is often ignored. In many ways, such a lack of focus is understandable, especially for those whose lives have not been spent within factory walls. The machine power that has emerged in the last century and a half is unquestionably impressive—it has changed the common metaphors of force, sensuality and purpose. In 1900, while visiting the Great Exposition in Paris, Henry Adams used words that characterize a transformation in beliefs which marks much thought about the modern "industrial revolution." While going through the Hall of Dynamos, Adams confronted these generators with a wonderment which he likened to that of early Christian fervor. The exposition which was showing off the great industrial achievements of the West was, for him, a sensuous and religious experience: ". . . to Adams the dynamo became a symbol of infinity. . . . he began to feel the forty foot dynamos as a moral force, much as the early Christians felt the cross. . . ."[1]

Within twentieth-century culture, the machine, the product of industrial development, has become a prevailing object of devotion as well, providing a common idiom of sensuality. In poetry, E. E. Cummings wrote of driving a car in terms which suggested the male defloration of a virgin woman—so hallowed a rite within our culture:

> she being Brand
>
> -new; and you
> know consequently a
> little stiff i was
> careful of her and (having

thoroughly oiled the universal
joint tested my gas felt of
her radiator made sure her springs were O.

K.) i went right to it flooded-the-carburetor cranked
   her
up, slipped the . . ."[2]

In the blues the interpenetration of sexuality and
the machine can be heard in the prescriptive line that
Sonny Terry and Brownie McGhee offer to an unresponsive woman:

Your motor ain't runnin,
so I better look under your hood.[3]

Such metaphors constitute a conspicuous part of American male language, and tell us the extent to which the
machine has come to stand for progress, power, and
sensuality.

Indeed the language of progress and of spiritual
and physical fulfillment permeates many perspectives
on industrialization. It is not surprising that mass consumption has been conceived of as an apotheosis of
human achievement: the wonder of the machine is
borne out in the modern infiltration of machine-made
goods into the lives and aspirations of people.

For many people, however, such a technologically
defined perspective does not convey a sense of their
own social experiences. Nor does it reflect the nature of
social relations, of power and of wealth that have
dominated the machine process in its development. For
many working people between the inception of industrial capitalism and World War I, the development of
factory production required an understanding less mys-
tical and less sanguine than that of Henry Adams.
Regarding those whose work and productive lives be-

came implicated in the realm of factory production, a focus on *proletarianization*—the shaping of people into a particularly *industrial* work force—may be a more pertinent means of describing our industrial history.

For working people, centuries of pre-industrial life (agricultural and artisan crafts) had created social rhythms and perceptions which the rationality of the factory system placed in a severe state of crisis. The work of E. P. Thompson in *The Making of the English Working Class* has vividly pictured the proletarianization of the working classes as a historic shock met with resistance and antagonism.[4] In the United States, industrial development may also be seen as a process of transforming the habits and life patterns of working people to conform to the conditions of the factory. Herbert G. Gutman, a leading student of American labor history, has observed that the proletarianization of the American population was particularly arduous and violent. Whereas in England the formation of the factory proletariat was a process of transforming a relatively homogeneous, mainly native population, the tension of that transformation in the United States was compounded by immigration—the source of the American labor force. Each successive immigrant group brought with it the perceptions of its particular non-industrial origins; each experienced the shock of factory life and each defended its own initiative against the mechanical rhythms of industrial rationality.[5]

Industrialization, then, was more than a question of producing more goods in a new way. It also entailed a process of socialization which aimed at stabilizing and inculcating fidelity among those whose labor was being conscripted. As Marx had perceived in his "Preface to a Contribution to the Critique of Political Economy," the modern "stage of development of [the] material powers of production" required the maintenance of specific and corresponding social formations and relations of production.[6] Within such a context, both Thompson and Gutman have described the ways in which religion, education, legislation and ultimately the use of military or police power became integrated in English and American society to insure the perpetuation of bourgeois and, later, corporate power within the industrial structure.

The issue of social control was an ongoing theme within the history of industrial capitalism. In the early stages of industrial development, at the beginning of the nineteenth century, the question of social control revolved mainly around the question of work. Nineteenth-century industrialists needed to mold an industrial work force to meet the necessities of capitalist production. The development and expansion of the industrial plant demanded a steady flow of workers whose work ability could be predicted and would therefore be reliable. The tension between this imperative and the dependence on people of non-industrial (often wageless) origins as a cheap labor supply was inevitable. While such people would work for less money than those who had been integrated into the industrial process, their work patterns stood in firm contradiction to the work demanded of them in the factory.

E. P. Thompson's brilliant social history of the clock—"Time, Work-Discipline, and Industrial Capitalism"—gives significant insight into the social textures of industrialization.[7] Focusing on the way in which industrialization necessitated a different sense of time than did non-industrial modes of production, Thompson has shown how the mechanical clock-time of the factory served as a transformative means of discipline. The clock was an assault against the time senses of people whose collective past had inculcated a time-perception based on seasons, movements of the sun and other categories of a predominantly agricultural society. Thompson's argument recognizes the primacy of the social reality which encompasses any productive process. Serving notice on those who would choose to view industrial history as technologically determined, he contends that "there is no such thing as economic growth which is not, at the same time, growth or change of a culture. . . ."[8] In his discussion of time, Thompson argues that the acclimatization of people to the mechanized work process required the implementation of a time-sense circumscribed by the divisions of mechanically produced rhythms. In other words, the machine mode of production could not be stabilized until it had also been socialized. The early history of industrialization was marked by tension between the workstyles workers brought into the early factory and those demanded within that mode of production; this conflict precipitated crises of wide-spread social unrest and violent clashes between workers and those employed to protect the interests of capital.[9]

Gutman demonstrates, as do contemporary sources, that much of the impulse behind working-class struggles during the nineteenth century came not around the issue of obtaining and maintaining a fit wage, but against the wage process itself. The cultural milieu of factory production appears to have been at the center of the crisis.[10] Within the labor movement, the feeling of immiserization and the political definition of poverty were not defined so much in terms of wage levels as they were by the quality of life within industry. Within the New England Eight-Hour Movement of the 1870s, for example, the definition of poverty was presented in terms of inequitable social relations. For industrial work as well as "white collar" or clerical wage earning, the Eight-Hour Movement assumed that the wage, regardless of its amount, was a means of oppression that robbed working people of the possibility of self-determination: hence the common labor definition of the wage as "wage-slavery."[11]

In the early years of the twentieth century, there was widespread working class resistance to industrial capitalism. While some workers looked to models in the pre-industrial past for solutions to their problems, by the end of the nineteenth century and certainly in the twentieth, the real issue that confronted them was the development of an industrial system which would be geared toward meeting people's needs; a system in which work and misery would no longer be synonymous. This was the goal of the Socialist Party under the standard of Eugene V. Debs, as well as that of the Industrial Workers of the World (IWW), groups of organized workers which went through a marked growth during the period. Both looked in the direction of an equitable society, committed to meeting the needs of its working population rather than conforming to the designs of wealthy industrialists.

In the period immediately following World War I, the appeal of anticapitalist politics among working people intensified. In 1919, within a relatively brief span of time, labor struggles erupted in fast succession. The Seattle General Strike, the Great Steel Strike, the United Mine Workers Strike in the coal fields, widespread demonstrations on May Day of 1919, and (perhaps the most alarming of all) a strike among the Boston Police Department brought about a brutal and characteristic response. In their wake came retaliatory raids, firings, repression, and massive deportation of immigrant workers and radicals. Some have chosen to view this period as a *momentary* madness, a "Red Scare."[12] In fact, the issues underlying the raids in the 1920s by Attorney General A. Mitchell Palmer and local police agencies against radical groups and workers were *characteristic* issues of industrial history in America, and were extensions of a broad attempt to create a stable work force which was faithful both to the conditions and relations of production.

During 1919 and throughout the twenties, the labor movement and unions lost organizational strength, while general social unrest continued. Interviews with working people of the time as well as articles in the labor press of the twenties indicate that the crises felt by working people were not being resolved by a strategy that equated social order with outright punitive enforcement. The response to the lack of self-determination among working people and the sense that industrial progress was not increasing their own social power was expressed by an Iowa meat-packing-plant employee in the late 1920s: "Things are better for us fellows than they used to be, but if a few people keep on getting the money, we'll be a bunch of fairly well-paid slaves."[13]

Vaughn Bachman Brokow, editor of the Sioux City *Union Advocate and Public Forum*, indicated that the issue of "wage-slavery" was far from settled. Speaking of the way in which the exchange process tied the worker within the profit system, Brokow offered the following interpretation:

> . . . our present kind of money, being supposed to be a medium of exchange, is a great deceiver, for its use leads people to suppose that they are exchanging when one is robbing and the other being robbed.[14]

While some unionists were already formulating the

demand for higher wages as their main goal,[15] Brokow maintained that the wage was a "means of appropriation" which forced workers to define their own survival in terms suitable to profiteers. To Brokow, the wage was not a fair or equitable means of exchange.[16]

Others in the labor ranks felt that factory life had become increasingly machine-defined, and that the industrial system was making them subservient to mechanically reproductive rhythms. Noting that once he and his boss had been on relatively friendly terms with each other, one industrial employee lamented that *now* (1928), "when they take anyone through the plant instead of introducing us men, they show 'em the new machinery."[17]

Even more telling is a feature article that appeared in the *Tri-City Labor Review* of Rock Island, Illinois. The story spoke to a central contradiction felt within modern industrial life: that as the factory increasingly produced what appeared to be the means to a better life, the social conditions within which goods were produced exposed the inequities guiding American industrialism:

> I ran into a fellow the other day who is waiting for one of the new Fords. "Nice car," he told me.
>
> But I always think about a visit I once paid to one of Ford's assembling plants every time any one mentions a Ford car to me. Every employee seemed to be restricted to a well-defined jerk, twist, spasm or quiver resulting in a fliver. I never thought it possible that human beings could be reduced to such perfect automats.
>
> I looked constantly for the wire or belt concealed about their bodies which kept them in motion with such marvelous clock-like precision. I failed to discover how the motive power is transmitted to these

people and as it don't seem reasonable that human beings would willingly consent to being simplified into jerks, I assume that their wives wind them up while asleep.

I shall never be able to look another Tin Lizzy in the face without shuddering at the memory of Henry's manikins. Some day when humanity has become more than an unavoidable adjunct to a machine, Henry Ford's process for the mass production of the Man with the Hoe will be shown in Museums of Unnatural History as a horrible example of what happened to the descendants of the ambitious ape who first used his fingers to make things, instead of using them to take things as the more intelligent of our race are still doing.[18]

A worker in the Ford assembly line in the late twenties gave concrete underpinning to the above bit of journalistic irony. The man spoke of how workers at Ford were being "driven by foremen picked for their brutality. . . . There was never a moment of leisure or opportunity to turn my head. . . . The men have no rest except for fifteen or twenty minutes at lunch time and can go to the toilet only when substitutes are ready to relieve them."[19]

The political attack on organized labor had effectively quieted much of the resistance of working people, yet the roots of that militancy were in the American industrial process itself. It was within this context that American industry began to produce a cultural apparatus aimed at defusing and neutralizing potential unrest.

The move in industrial thought was in the direction of "human management"—a more affirmative approach to discipline. Thomas Edison, whose popular image as a workshop tinkerer obscures his leadership in establishing modern corporate research laboratories, was acutely aware of the need for a change in business's methods of

social control. Writing critically of the punitive tradition
of industrial order, Edison commented that early
"American business civilization was raw and crude,
pretty wasteful, pretty cruel, which often comes to the
same thing. . . . Our production, our factory laws, our
charities, our relations between capital and labor [are]
all wrong, out of gear. We've stumbled along for a while
trying to run a new civilization in old ways, but we've got
to start to make this world over."[20]

Increasingly businessmen confronted the question
of industrial management in terms which coordinated
the manipulation of material resources with a systematic
approach to handling the work force. The "science" of
human engineering was coming to the fore as an
industrial concern. The implementation of the time-
motion studies of Frederick W. Taylor and others
attested to the new interaction of business and the social
sciences in confronting the problem of making an often
antagonistic work force behave stably and predictably.[21]
In 1915 and 1916 the American Academy of Political
and Social Science devoted two numbers of its *Annals* to
the problem of managing employees. The thrust behind professionalizing manpower management is neatly
contained in a statement by Meyer Bloomfield, the
director of the Vocational Bureau of Boston, and a local
business leader. "The biggest of all industrial problems," he declared in 1915, "is the problem of handling
men." Conceding that traditional approaches to social
discipline had failed to quell social antagonism to capitalism, Bloomfield re-emphasized the industrial "goal of
welding the working force into a stable, dependable and
well-assimilated organization," adding that "such organization is rare in modern industry."[22] Social Science
was offering its tools as a means of rectifying the
situation.

The crisis of social control was a broad theme of

industrial thought. By 1917 *System*, a business journal concerned with the rationalization of the productive system, was presenting the problems of "management in the nude," shorn of its scientistic rhetoric. These problems surrounded the primary concern of "supervising and conserving the business." Presenting a structural schema for industrial planning, *System* argued that the question of "handling the help" was central to business survival, a more volatile and difficult consideration than "analyzing the job," "planning the operations" or "organizing the work." The issue of neutralizing social unrest had emerged as a strategic concern in the minds of people whose predecessors had relied on a less systematic approach for maintaining industrial order.[23]

The need to produce pacific social relations was appearing more and more as part of the agenda for modern management. It was felt that pacified social relations could be the products of the industrial process. Such a development moved away from a conception of workers merely in their productive capacity, toward an increased delving into their properties as social and psychological beings. With mass production, management entered a period in which workers began to be considered as potential "citizens" of a new industrial civilization, rather than merely "wheelhorses" in the productive process. Mass production, after all, pointed to a disengagement of the "wheelhorse" proletarian from much of his work. So too did its growing productivity point toward a need for markets which transcended the traditional boundaries of industrial-goods consumption. The consolidation of the productive system in the nineteenth century bore fruit in the twentieth. A retooling of worker-industry relationships was seen as necessary. Such a retooling was not to be in the area of redefining control over industry, but was directed more toward redefining the arenas in which workers might commit themselves to the industrial process. The growth of goods production offered a context in which industrial discipline might more and more come to define the realm of consumption as well as that of production. It was at this juncture that the character of proletarianization began to change.

The shifting sense of social control among industrialists can be seen in the development of worker safety and recreation programs, representing concessions won by the labor movement as well as new arenas of ideological input for modern industry. The so-called "welfare programs" which began to appear in the post-1910 period were instituted by industries and seen as a means of stabilizing the work force. At International Harvester, Ford, and U.S. Steel, welfare programs were implemented before 1920. While aspects of these programs were directed at offering forms of recreation to workers, they were for the most part concerned with making people work more diligently. The programs included language and civics classes for immigrant workers. The content of these classes was mainly oriented toward industrial discipline. Significantly, Gertrude Beeks, a founder of such programs, noted that in the interest of inculcating factory order "'the so-called democratic idea' should be avoided" within such classes.[24]

As the notion of control expanded, the ways in which working people might be involved in the industrial process beyond their factory role became increasingly explored. The studies of early twentieth-century social scientists and "Progressive" social critics began to create a general understanding that the social control of workers must stretch beyond the realm of the factory and into the very communities and structures within which they lived. As early as 1910, the *Pittsburgh Survey*, a broad sociological study funded by the Russell Sage Foundation, had underwritten the concept of capitalism as more than a system of production; it was in fact a social system in which the family, community, and the means or lack of means for recreation and pleasure were undergoing a severe crisis.

In her volume of the *Pittsburgh Survey* on the steel-mill town of Homestead, Pennsylvania, Margaret Byington emphasized that the corporate structure of Carnegie Steel was having a tremendous impact on the social lives of people beyond the particular arena of work. Children's recreation had been limited to the cramped shadows of the mill; the town, which was "almost entirely dependent on the outsiders who own these industries," had "no provision for their simplest recreational needs in the scheme of things."[25] Describing the social reality of the households of Homestead (both native and immigrant laborers), Byington focused on a basic contradiction of industrial social life which had long been felt by working people, but which only recently had concerned those who held the reigns of industrial power:

> The setting of the average Homestead household is now fairly complete before us. On the one hand is the inexorable mill, offering wages and work under such conditions as it pleases; on the other, is a town politically failing to maintain a sound environment for its inhabitants and not possessed of . . . resources sufficient to serve them.[26]

While the people of Homestead continued to attempt to maintain their own indigenous cultural life, the industrial reality was clearly impinging on such an impulse. As working families continued to do subsistence gar-

dening and other "home industries" alongside their
industrial tasks, the housing and social space of the town
was becoming decreasingly able to sustain such activities. As people attempted to set aside parlors for family
life and activities with neighbors, the hours of work
were such that they cut significantly into the patterns of
social interaction which people desired.[27] Byington
wrote of how the shifts within the steel mill were such
that they required an irregularity of meals, making
"hospitality difficult,"[28] and of how the working family
fought hard to maintain an "atmosphere that the children might find their happiness in the home rather
than seek it in the doubtful amusements [nickelodeons
and skating rinks] the town offers". The main source
of town entertainment in Homestead was in the library, "on the high ground of Munhill," too distant a
walk for those living tired in the lower boroughs of
Homestead.[29] To those who would uncritically praise
the wonder of modern industry, Byington answers
resoundingly:

> The onlooker, fascinated by the picturesqueness of it
> all, sees in the great dim sheds a wonderful revelation
> of the creative powers of man. To the worker, this
> fascination is gone; heat and grime, noise and effort
> are his part in the play.[30]

The institution of "welfare" programs by business
as well as its increased reliance on the social and
psychological sciences cannot be separated from the
social dimension of the crisis that was developing in
which the involvement of workers in overtly anticapitalist
politics was seriously threatening the locus of power
within industry.

Speaking for businessmen in the Boston area (1915),
Meyer Bloomfield noted that "the new profession of

handling men" must transcend the question of organizing the plant, and move toward a vision of rationalization aimed at the communities in which working people lived. Arguing for an implementation of a social capitalism, Bloomfield stated that "wise business management recognizes the good sense of organizing the *source of labor supply*" beyond the immediacy of the factory. (My emphasis.)[31] This perspective was linked to changes in the productive capacity of American business—the fact that for the first time it appeared that the industrial machine might be able to transform the nature of consumption among a broad sector of the population.

It was within such a context that the advertising industry began to assume modern proportions and that the institution of a *mass* consumer market began to arise. Up to that point, much of indigenous working-class culture had resisted capitalist growth in general, and the invasion of capitalism into their work and lifestyles in particular. The factory had not been an effective arena for forging a predictable and reliable work force. More and more it appeared that proletarian integration might be effected within the realm opened up by increased productivity and the need for broader markets. The juncture of working-class resentment and the expansion of productivity called for a vision of social order in which the two might operate integrally rather than at odds with one another. The imposition of factory discipline, characteristic of American industrialization up to that point, had not been an entirely effective means toward confronting the unrest born of its routines. As a result, the business community now attempted to present an affirmative vision—a new mechanism—of social order in the realm of daily life to confront the resistance of people whose work lives were increasingly defined by the rigid parameters of industrial production and their corporate bureaucracies.

Before we turn to the particular history of advertising and consumption in the 1920s, certain things must be said. True, advertising was to develop as a tool of social order whose self-espoused purpose was the "nullification" of the "customs of ages; [to] . . . break down the barriers of individual habits." It defined itself as "at once the destroyer and creator in the process of the ever-evolving new. Its constructive effort [was] . . . to superimpose new conceptions of individual attainment and community desire"; to solidify the productive process while at the same time parrying anticorporate feeling.[32] Beyond standing at the helm of the industrial machines, businessmen understood the social nature of their hegemony. They looked to move beyond their nineteenth-century characterization as captains of industry toward a position in which they could control the entire social realm. They aspired to become captains of consciousness. Yet at the same time it must be said that this imperative was constrained within the strictures of economic possibility. In the 1920s the consumer ethic was projected to sectors of the population whose fidelity was seen to be necessary, but in the process much of the American populace was ignored. Ads of the twenties, like the mass consumer market itself, were not generally directed toward the poorest sectors of the population. The development of an ideology of consumption responded both to the issue of social control and the need for goods distribution. It reflected the limits and possibilities of its history. Clearly, while the phenomena discussed in the following sections significantly altered the cultural atmosphere of American society in the twenties, its success was limited then, as it is today, by its ability to deliver that which it promised. The developments of advertising and mass markets did not bring the social crisis of industrialization to an end. They altered its course and its meaning within people's lives.

ONE
Advertising as Social Production

Consumptionism is the name given to the new doctrine; and it is admitted today to be the greatest idea that America has to give to the world; the idea that workmen and masses be looked upon not simply as workers and producers, but as *consumers*. . . . Pay them more, sell them more, prosper more is the equation.

—MRS. CHRISTINE FREDERICK,
Selling Mrs. Consumer (1929)

1 "Shorter hours, higher wages . . ."

In 1910, Henry Ford instituted the "line production system" for "maximum production economy" in his Highland Park, Michigan, plant.[1] The innovation, though in many ways unsophisticated, and hardly educated as to its own implications, was the beginning of a momentous transformation in America's capacity to produce. In quantitative terms, the change was staggering. On the 1910 line, the time required to assemble a chassis was twelve hours and twenty-eight minutes. "By spring of 1914, the Highland Park plant was turning out over 1,000 vehicles a day, and the average labor time for assembling a chassis had dropped to one hour and thirty-three minutes."[2]

Mass production was a way of making production more economical. Through his use of the assembly line, Ford was able to utilize "expensive, single-purpose" machinery along with "quickly trained, single-purpose" workmen to make a single-model, inexpensive automobile at a rate which, with increasing sophistication, continued to dwarf not only the production levels of premassified industry, but the output of less refined mass production systems.[3]

By the 1920s, interest in and employment of the industrial potential of mass production extended far beyond the automobile industry. In recognition of such industrial developments, the United States Special Census of 1921 and 1923 offered a study of productive capacity[4] which was one of the first general discussions of its kind.[5] Consumer goods manufacturers were coming to recognize that mass production and mass distribution were "necessary" steps toward survival in a competitive market. Edward Filene, of the Boston department store family, a businessman founder of the consumer union movement, articulated the competitive compulsion of mass production. Competition, said Filene, "will compel us to Fordize American business and industry."[6]

And yet, what Filene and others meant by "Fordizing" American industry transcended the myopic vision of Henry Ford. While Ford stubbornly held to the notion that "the work and the work *alone* controls us,"[7] others in the automobile industry[8] and, (for our purposes) more importantly, ideologues of mass industry outside of the auto industry viewed the strategy of production in far broader social terms. Before mass production, industry had produced for a limited, largely middle- and upper-class market. With a burgeoning productive capacity, industry now required an equivalent increase in potential consumers of its goods. "Scientific production promised to make the conventional notion of the self-reliant producer/consumer anachronistic."[9]

The mechanism of mass production could not function unless markets became more dynamic, growing horizontally (nationally), vertically (into social classes not previously among the consumers) and ideologically. Now men and women had to be habituated to respond to the demands of the productive machinery. The corollary to a freely growing system of goods production was a "systematic, nationwide plan . . . to endow the masses with more buying power," a freely growing system of consumer production.[10] The modern mass producer could not depend upon an elite market to respond to his productive capacity. From a dependence upon local markets or localized markets scattered nationally,[11] the manufacturer was forced to "count on the whole United States if he [was] . . . going to manufacture a large enough quantity of goods to reduce the cost to the point where he [could] . . . compete with other manufacturers of the same goods"[12] and subsequently distribute his mass produced wares more efficiently and profitably. He was required to create an ideological bridge across traditional social gaps—region, taste, need and class—which would narrow prejudices in his favor.

Considering the quantitative possibilities of mass production, the question of "national markets" became one of qualitatively changing the nature of the American buying public. In response to the exigencies of the productive system of the twentieth century, excessiveness replaced thrift as a social value. It became imperative to invest the laborer with a financial power and a psychic desire to consume.

By the end of the depression of 1921, "productive machinery was so effective that even more so than before much greater markets were absolutely necessary than those provided by the existing public buying power."[13] As the question of expanding old and creating new markets became a function of the massification of industry, foresighted businessmen began to see the necessity of organizing their businesses not merely around the production of goods, but around the creation of a buying public. "The changes that we shall be obliged to make in production," noted Filene, "will lead to pretty thorough overhauling of our machinery and methods of distribution, and, in the end, both the quantity and quality of consumption will be dictated by them."[14] As the "twentieth-century industrialist . . . realized to a greater extent than did his predecessors, that he must understand the living world contained by his factory,"[15] so too did he realize that he must understand and manipulate, as part of his productive apparatus, the total world occupied by his workers. The necessity to "influence human conduct," the knowledge that goods production meant social production, encoded within the rhetoric of some businessmen a revealing idiom; "human conduct" or the "consumer's dollar" became equivalent to industrial discoveries, more valuable to manufacturing "than the uses of electricity or steel."[16] Within an ideal of a "scientifically" managed industry, raw materials and consumers were both viewed as malleable. They both would have to be shaped by the demands of the production line, pecuniary interests, and the newly emergent managerial tools of capital.

As capitalism became characterized by mass production and the subsequent need for mass distribution, traditional expedients for the real or attempted manipulation of labor were transformed. While the nineteenth-century industrialist coerced labor (both on and off the job) to serve as the "wheelhorse" of industry, modernizing capitalism sought to change "wheelhorse" to "worker" and "worker" to "consumer."[17]

For the workers, the movement toward mass production had severely changed the character of labor. The worker had become a decreasingly "significant" unit of production within the modern manufacturing process. "The man who had been the more or less creative maker of the whole of an article became the tender of a machine that made only one small part of the article."[18] The time required to teach the worker the "adept performance" of his "operation on assembly work" was a matter of a few hours.[19] This development had significant repercussions both in terms of the way in which a laborer viewed his proletarian status and in terms of the manufacturer's need to mass distribute the mountainous fruits of mass production. The two phenomena merged in the redefinition of the proletarian status. While mass production defined labor's work in terms of monotony and rationalized its product to a fragment, some businessmen spoke of "economic freedom" or "industrial democracy"[20] as the blessing promised the worker by modern production methods. Yet the "freedom" and "democracy" offered by mass industry stopped short of a freedom to define the uses or to rearrange the relationships of production. "The industrial democracy I am discussing," Filene assured those who might fear its anticapitalist implications, "has nothing to do with the Cubist politics of class revolution."[21] What was meant, rather, was that modern industrial production required that workers be free to "cultivate themselves" among the uncontestable fruits of the new industrial cornucopia.

The endowment of the masses with "industrial democracy" was seen as a complex and involving process. Their traditional role in capitalism had afforded them neither the cash nor the conviction to be so "democratized." It was imperative that the worker "desire a larger share in the mental and spiritual satisfactions of the property of his daily job much more than . . . *a larger share in the management of the enterprise which furnishes that job*."[22]

Not only was this alleged democracy designed to define the modern worker as a smoothly running unit of industrial production, it also tended to define protest and proletarian unrest in terms of the desire to consume, making these profitable as well. By the demand of workers for the right to be better consumers, the aspirations of labor would be profitably coordinated with the aspirations of capital. Such convictions implicitly attempted to divest protest of its anticapitalist content. Modern labor protest should have no basis in class antagonism.[23]

By the twenties, the ideological vanguard of the business community saw the need to endow the masses with what the economic historian Norman Ware has called the money, commodity, and psychic wages (satisfactions) correlative and responsive to the route of industrial capitalism.[24] There was a dramatic movement toward objective conditions which would make mass consumption feasible: higher wages and shorter hours. Giving official sanction to such visions, Herbert Hoover noted that "High wages [are the] . . . very essence of great production."[25] In 1923, Julius Barnes, president of the U.S. Chamber of Commerce, spoke of the need to *prevent* the overconcentration of wealth, which threatened the development of a "broad purchasing market necessary to absorb our production."[26] Certainly the movement to higher wages preceded the twenties, but it is mainly in the twenties that this movement became linked to a general strategy to consumerize the worker. As early as 1914, Henry Ford had instituted the five-dollar work-day wage, but his innovation coexisted with a nineteenth-century Protestant value system which the worker was expected to maintain.[27] This system significantly clashed with the "economic freedom" that, out of necessity, attempted to subvert the moderation earlier valued for the masses.

The question of shorter hours was also tantamount to offering labor the "chance" to expand the consumer market. And yet, this notion of "chance," like the notions of "industrial democracy" and "economic freedom," were subterfuges in so much as these alleged freedoms and choices meant merely a transformed version of capitalism's incessant need to mold a work force in its own image. "As modern industry ... [was] geared to mass production, time out for mass consumption becomes as much a necessity as time in for production."[28] The shortening of hours was seen as a qualita tive as well as quantitative change in the worker's life, without significantly altering his relation to power over the uses and means of production. In addition to increasing the amount of leisure, it was hoped that shorter hours would productively determine "to some extent, the use of leisure and consumption. . . ."[29] Shorter hours and higher wages were seen as a first step in a broader offensive against notions of thrift and an attempt to habituate a national population to the exigencies of mass production. A capitalism that had previously required the worker to "live, move, and . . . [have] . . his being *there on the job*"[30] was now, in some industries, trying to undo such notions. Now priorities demanded that the worker spend his wages and leisure time on the consumer market. Realizing that earlier conditions had not been "favorable to such a worker's finding in, say, the sector of his home the sought-for satisfactions of forward movement and distinction," Whiting Williams, personnel director for a steel company and an ideologue of "scientific" management, felt that labor had developed a "suspicion" of such "sought-for satisfactions." Once again linking the rhetoric of freedom to the necessities of capitalism, Filene noted that,

> modern workmen have learned their habits of consumption and their habits of spending (thrift) in the

OUACHITA TECHNICAL COLLEGE

school of fatigue, in a time when high prices and relatively low wages have made it necessary to spend all the energies of the body and mind in providing food, clothing and shelter. We have no right to be overcritical of the way they spend a new freedom or a new prosperity until they have had as long a training in the school of freedom.[31]

Within the vision of consumption as a "school of freedom," the entry onto the consumer market was described as a "civilizing" experience. "Civilization" was the expanded cultural world which flowed from capitalism's broad capacity to commodify material resources. The experience of civilization was the cultural world this capacity produced.

And yet the "school of freedom" posed various problems. The democratic terminology within which the profitable vision of consumption was posed did not reveal the social and economic realities that threatened that vision. In terms of economic development, the financial growth of industrial corporations averaged 286 percent between 1922 and 1929. Despite wage hikes and relatively shorter hours in some industries,[32] the average manufacturing wage-earner showed a wage increase of only 14 percent during this same period.[33] The discrepancy between purchasing power and the rate of industrial growth was dealt with in part by the significant development of installment selling[34] which grew as an attempt to bolster "inadequate" markets in the economically depressed years of the early twenties.

Despite the initiation of a corporate credit system which offered consumers supplementary money, the growth of the productive system forced many industrial ideologues to realize the continuous need to habituate people psychically to consumption beyond mere changes in the productive order which they inhabited.

2 Mobilizing the Instincts

The man with the proper imagination is able to conceive of any commodity in such a way that it becomes an object of emotion to him and to those to whom he imparts his picture, and hence creates desire rather than a mere feeling of ought.[35]

—WALTER DILL SCOTT,
Influencing Men in Business (1911)

Modern advertising must be seen as a direct response to the needs of mass industrial capitalism. Second in procession after the manager of the production line, noted Whiting Williams, "came the leader who possessed the ability to develop and direct men's desires and demands in a way to furnish the organized mass sales required for the mass production made possible by the massed dollars."[36] Advertising, as a part of mass distribution within modernizing industries, became a major sector for business investment. Within the automobile industry, initiated by the broad and highly

31

diversified G.M. oligopoly, distribution came to account for about one half of that investment. Among producers of smaller consumer goods, the percentage of capital devoted to product proliferation was often greater.[37]

In the 1920s, advertising played a role of growing significance in industry's attempt to develop a continually responsive consumer market. Although committed national corporations saw advertising as an invaluable component of critical economic planning,[38] its acceptance was hardly universal. In its early days the mass advertising industry that developed in concert with the mass needs of industrial corporations continually had to sell itself to industry. Between 1918 and 1923, a greater percentage of articles in the advertising trade journal *Printers' Ink*, were devoted to ways of convincing "ancient" corporations that advertising was a given of modern industrialism than were devoted to advertising and merchandising techniques. During the 1920s, however, advertising grew to the dimensions of a major industry. In 1918, total gross advertising revenues in general and farm magazines was $58.5 million. By 1920 the gross had reached $129.5 million; and by 1929, $196.3 million. Such figures do not include newspaper revenues or, more significantly, direct-to-buyer advertising, which still comprised a major, though declining, sector of the industry.

In an address to the American Association of Advertising Agencies on October 27, 1926, Calvin Coolidge noted that the industry now required "for its maintenance, investments of great capital, the occupation of large areas of floor space, the employment of an enormous number of people."[39] The production line had insured the efficient creation of vast quantities of consumer goods; now ad men spoke of their product as "business insurance"[40] for profitable and efficient distribution of these goods. While line management tended to the process of goods production, social management (advertisers) hoped to make the cultural milieu of capitalism as efficient as line management had made production. Their task was couched in terms of a secular religion for which the advertisers sought adherents. Calvin Coolidge, applauding this new clericism, noted that "advertising ministers to the spiritual side of trade."[41]

Advertising offered itself as a means of efficiently creating consumers and as a way of homogeneously "controlling the consumption of a product."[42] Although many corporations boasted of having attained national markets without the aid of advertising, the trade journal *Printers' Ink* argued that these "phantom national markets" were actually inefficient, unpredictable and scattered agglomerations of heterogeneous local markets.[43] The significance of the notion of efficiency in the creation of consumers lies in the fact that the modern advertising industry, like the modern manufacturing plant, was an agent of consolidated and multi-leveled commerce. As Ford's assembly line utilized "expensive single-purpose machinery" to produce automobiles inexpensively and at a rate that dwarfed traditional methods, the costly machinery of advertising that Coolidge had described set out to produce consumers, likewise inexpensively and at a rate that dwarfed traditional methods. To create consumers efficiently the advertising industry had to develop universal notions of what makes people respond, going beyond the "horse sense" psychology that had characterized the earlier industry.[44] Such general conceptions of human instinct promised to provide ways of reaching a mass audience via a universal appeal. Considering the task of having to build a mass ad industry to attend to the needs of mass production, the ad men welcomed the work of psychologists in the articulation of these general conceptions.[45]

The vanguard of the business community found the social psychology of such men as Floyd Henry Allport extremely useful in giving an ideological cohesion to much of what one sees in the advertising of the twenties.[46] Explicating his notion of the way in which man develops a sense of himself from infancy, Allport asserted that "our consciousness of ourselves is largely a reflection of the consciousness which others have of us. . . . My idea of myself is rather my own idea of my neighbor's view of me."[47] This notion of the individual as the object of continual and harsh social scrutiny underscored the argument of much of the ad texts of the decade.

Whether or not the general conception of "self" as propounded by Floyd Henry Allport had a direct bearing on the *Weltanschauung* held by advertising in the 1920s is not clear. It was generally conceded, however, that a "knowledge of people—human nature"[48]—was as necessary a constituent of social production as the line manager's knowledge of his raw materials was to goods production.

While agreeing that "human nature is more difficult to control than material nature,"[49] ad men spoke in specific terms of "human instincts" which if properly understood could induce people "to buy a given product if it was scientifically presented. If advertising copy appealed to the right instincts, the urge to buy would surely be excited."[50] The utilitarian value of a product or the traditional notion of mechanical quality were no longer sufficient inducements to move merchandise at the necessary rate and volume required by mass production.

Such traditional appeals would not change the disposition of potential markets toward consumption of given products. Instead each product would be offered in isolation, not in terms of the nature of the consumer, but through an argument based on the intrinsic qualities of the item itself.

The advertisers were concerned with effecting a self-conscious change in the psychic economy, which could not come about if they spent all their time talking about a product and none talking about the "reader." Advertising literature, following the advent of mass production methods, increasingly spoke in terms of appeals to instinct. Anticipating later implementation, by 1911, Walter Dill Scott, psychologist/author of *Influencing Men in Business*, noted that "goods offered as means of gaining social prestige make their appeals to one of the most profound of the human instincts."[51] Yet the instinct for "social prestige," as well as others of a broad "constellation"[52] of instincts, was channeled into the terms of the productive system. The use value of "prestige," of "beauty," of "acquisition," of "self-adornment," and of "play" were all placed in the service of advertising's basic purpose—to provide effective mass distribution of products. Carl A. Naether, an advocate of advertising for women, demonstrated how the link might be effected between "instinct" and mass sales.

> An attractive girl admiring a string of costly pearls just presented to her would in no few cases make the one seeing her in an advertisement exclaim: "I wish that *I, too,* might have a set of these pearls and so enhance my personal appearance." Such and similar longings are merely expressions of real or fancied need for what is advertised.[53]

The creation of "fancied need" was crucial to the modern advertiser. The transcendence of traditional consumer markets and buying habits required people to

buy, not to satisfy their own fundamental needs, but
rather to satisfy the real, historic needs of capitalist
productive machinery. Advertising was a way of making
people put time and energy into what Calvin Coolidge
referred to as their "education"[54] to production. The
investment of time and energy in deliberation over an
advertisement, as described by Scott,[55] enacted in microcosm the commitment of one's total time and energy
to consumption. Advertising demanded but a momentary participation in the logic of consumption. Yet
hopefully that moment would be expanded into a life
style by its educational value. A given ad asked not only
that an individual buy its product, but that he experience a self-conscious perspective that he had previously
been socially and psychically denied. By that perspective, he could ameliorate social and personal frustrations through access to the marketplace.

In light of such notions as Allport's "social self" and
other self-objectifying visions of popularity and success,[56] a new cultural logic was projected by advertising
beyond the strictly pecuniary one of creating the desire
to consume. The social perception was one in which
people ameliorated the negative condition of social
objectification through consumption—material objectification. The negative condition was portrayed as social
failure derived from continual public scrutiny. The
positive goal emanated from one's *modern* decision to
armor himself against such scrutiny with the accumulated "benefits" of industrial production. Social responsibility and social self-preservation were being correlated
to an allegedly existential decision that one made to
present a mass-produced public face. Man, traditionally
seen as exemplary of God's perfect product, was now
hardly viable in comparison with the man-made products of industrial expertise. The elevation of man's

works in the cosmos which had underlined the half-way covenant among New England Puritans was now being secularized into the realm of mass social production. It was felt that capitalism, through an appeal to instincts—ultimately feelings of social insecurity—could habituate men and women to consumptive life.[57] Such social production of consumers represented a shift in social and political priorities which has since characterized much of the "life" of American industrial capitalism. The functional goal of national advertising was the creation of desires and habits. In tune with the need for mass distribution that accompanied the development of mass production capabilities, advertising was trying to produce in readers personal needs which would dependently fluctuate with the expanding marketplace.

Exposing an affirmative vision of capitalist production, Calvin Coolidge reassured the members of the ad industry in 1926 that "rightfully applied, it [advertising] is the method by which the desire is created for better things."[58] The nature of this desire, and not incidentally the nature of capitalism, required an unquestioning attitude toward the uses of production. The use of psychological methods, therefore, attempted to turn the consumer's critical functions away from the product and toward himself. The determining factor for buying was self-critical and ideally ignored the intrinsic worth of the product. The Lynds, in their study, *Middletown*, noted that unlike ads of a generation before, modern advertising was

> concentrating increasingly upon a type of copy aiming to make the reader emotionally uneasy, to bludgeon him with the fact that decent people don't live the way he does. . . . This copy points an accusing finger at the stenographer as she reads her motion picture magazine and makes her acutely conscious of her

> unpolished finger nails . . . and sends the housewife
> peering anxiously into the mirror to see if her wrin-
> kles look like those that made Mrs. X in the advertise-
> ment "old at thirty-five" because she did not have a
> Leisure Hour electric washer.[59]

Advertising hoped to elicit the "instinctual" anxieties
of social intercourse. Cutex Hand Preparations made of
well-tended hands an armor against failure. Hoping to
prepare the psyche for such an argument, Cutex advertisements declared in the *Ladies' Home Journal*, April
1920:

> You will be amazed to find how many times in one
> day people glance at your nails. At each glance a
> judgment is made. . . . Indeed some people make a
> practice of basing their estimate of a new acquaint-
> ance largely upon this one detail.

Even those whose physical appearances were market-
ably "safe," who appeared to be "the picture of health,"
were warned of the inscrutable perils with which they
traveled. Listerine was offered as an agent to militate
against "The Hidden Wells of Poison" that lurk and
conspire against the "program[s] of pleasure" of even
the most beautiful women.

The Lynds saw advertising "and other channels of
increased cultural diffusion from without . . . [as] rap-
idly changing habits of thought as to what things are
essential to living and multiplying optional occasions for
spending money."[60] The critical analysis offered by the
Lynds found unwitting support in predominant advertising theory. It was recognized that in order to get
people to consume and, more importantly, to keep
them consuming, it was more efficient to endow them
with a critical self-consciousness in tune with the
"solutions" of the marketplace than to fragmentarily

argue for products on their own merit. Writing in *Printers' Ink*, Frederick P. Anderson spoke of the industry's conscious attempt to direct man's critical faculties against himself or his environment, "to make him self-conscious about matter of course things such as enlarged nose pores, bad breath. . . ."[61]

In mass advertising, the consciousness of a selling point was precisely the theorized "self-consciousness" of the modern consumer which had occasioned the Lynds' remarks.[62] This consumer self-consciousness was clearly identifiable with the continuous need for product proliferation that informed modern industry. Linking the theories of "self-consciousness" to the exigencies of capitalism, one writer in *Printers' Ink* commented that "advertising helps to keep the masses dissatisfied with their mode of life, discontented with *ugly things* around them. Satisfied customers are not as profitable as discontented ones."[63]

3 Advertising: Civilizing the *Self*

In his sympathetic book ‚on the *History and Development of Advertising*, Frank Presbrey articulated the conception of a predictable, buying, national population in proud and patriotic terms. "To National Advertising," noted Presbrey, "has recently been attributed most of the growth of a national homogeneity in our people, a uniformity of ideas which, despite the mixture of races, is found to be greater here than in European countries whose population is made up almost wholly of people of one race and would seem easier to nationalize in all respects."[64] Presbrey's conception of "national homogeneity" was a translucent reference to what Calvin Coolidge saw as "the enormous capacity for consumption of all kinds of commodities which characterizes our country."[65]

The idea that advertising was producing a homogeneous national character was likened within the trade as a "civilizing influence comparable in its cultural effects to those of other great epoch-making developments in history."[66] Yet not all of the conceptions of advertising were expressed in such epic and transhistorical terminology. Sensitive to the political and economic context of such notions as "civilizing," "national homogeneity" and "capacity for consumption," William Allen White bridged the gap between "civilization" and civil society, noting that modern advertising was particularly a formation of advanced capitalist production. Aiming his critique at internal and external "revolutionist" threats to capitalism, White turned contemporary conceptions of revolution on their head. Reasserting the efficacy of the American Revolutionary tradition, he argued that advertising men were the true "revolutionists." Juxtaposing the consumer market to revolution of a socialistic variety, White presented a satirical political strategy to halt the "golden quest" for consumer goods. "I would cut out the advertising and fill the editorial and news pages with material supplied by communists and reds. That would stop buying—distribution of things. It would bring an impasse in civilization, which would immediately begin to decay."[67] Identifying ad men with the integrity and survival of the American heritage, White numbered advertising among our sacred cultural institutions.

Through advertising, then, consumption took on a clearly cultural tone. Within governmental and business rhetoric, consumption assumed an ideological veil of nationalism and democratic lingo. The mass "American type," which defined unity on the bases of common ethnicity, language, class or literature, was ostensibly born out of common desires—mass responses to the demands of capitalist production. Mass industry, requiring a corresponding mass individual, cryptically named him "Civilized American" and implicated his national heritage in the marketplace. By defining himself and his desires in terms of the good of capitalist production, the worker would implicitly accept the foundations of modern industrial life. By transforming the notion of "class" into "mass," business hoped to create an "individual" who could locate his needs and frustrations in terms of the consumption of goods rather than the quality and content of his life (work).

Advertisements aimed at transforming pockets of resistance contained the double purpose of sales and "civilization." Resistance to the "universal" appeals of modern advertising was often dealt with in racial or national terms. In an article referring to immigrant readers of the domestic foreign language press, a writer in *Printers' Ink* noted that these *less American* elements of the population had not yet been sophisticated to the methods of modern advertising. While other Americans were portrayed as responding to appeals to universal instinct, the author noted that "Swedes and Germans . . . study the most minute detail of anything they consider buying."[68] It was felt that a particular form of advertising had to be developed to temporarily accommodate immigrant and other defined resistance to nationalization. While it was suggested that for immediate sales, ads could be written offering extensive proof of a product's intrinsic worth, other forms of advertising assumed the task of the "democratization" which Edward Filene had exalted. "Antidote advertising" and other, less theoretical tactics were designed to repudiate antique beliefs which had no place in *the social style* of modern industrial life. Often, such ads were geared to make people ashamed of their origins and, consequently, the habits and practices that betrayed them as alien. The Sherwin Cody School of English advertised that a less-than-perfect mastery of the language was *just* cause for social ostracism. "If someone you met for the first time made . . . mistakes in English . . . What would you think of him? Would he inspire your respect? Would you be inclined to make a friend of him? Would you care to introduce him to others as a close friend of yours?"[69] Rather than arguing that a knowledge of the language would be helpful in conversation and effective communication, the ad argued that being distinguishable from the fabricated national norm, a part of advertising's mythologized homogeneity, was a justification for social failure.

In an attempt to massify men's consumption in step with the requirements of the productive machinery, advertising increasingly offered mass-produced solutions to "instinctive" strivings as well as to the ills of mass society itself. If it was industrial capitalism around which crowded cities were being built and which had spawned much of the danger to health, the frustration, the loneliness and the insecurity of modern industrial life, the advertising of the period denied complicity. Rather, the logic of contemporaneous advertising read, one can free oneself from the ills of modern life by embroiling oneself in the maintenance of that life. A 1924 ad for Pompeian facial products argued that

> unless you are one woman in a thousand, you must use powder and rouge. Modern living has robbed women of much of their natural color . . . taken away the conditions that once gave natural roses in the cheeks.[70]

Within such literature, the term "modern living" was an ahistorical epithet, devoid of the notion "Modern Industrial Society," and teeming with visions of the benefits of civilization which had emerged, one would think, quite apart from the social conditions and relations to which these "benefits" therapeutically addressed themselves. On the printed page, modern living was defined as heated houses, easy transportation, and the conveniences of the household. To the reader it may have meant something considerably different: light-starved housing, industrial pollution, poor nutrition, boredom. In either sense, modern life offered the same sallow skin and called for a solution through consumption. Within such advertisements, business called for a transformation of the critique of bourgeois society to an implicit commitment to that society.

The advertising which attempted to create the dependable mass of consumers required by modern industry often did so by playing upon the fears and frustrations evoked by mass society—offering mass produced visions of individualism by which people could extricate themselves from the mass. The rationale was simple. If a person was unhappy within mass industrial society, advertising was attempting to put that unhappiness to work in the name of that society.

In an attempt to boost mass sales of soap, the Cleanliness Institute, a cryptic front group for the soap and glycerine producers' association, pushed soap as a "Kit for Climbers" (social, no doubt). The illustration was a multitudinous mountain of men, each climbing over one another to reach the summit. At the top of this indistinguishable mass stood one figure, his arms outstretched toward the sun, whose rays spelled out the words "Heart's Desire." The ad cautioned that "in any path of life, that long way to the top is hard enough—so make the going easier with soap and water." In an attempt to build a responsive mass market, the Cleanliness Institute appealed to what they must have known was a major dissatisfaction with the reality of mass life. Their solution was a sort of mass pseudo-demassification.

A good deal of drug and toilet goods advertising made even more specific references to the quality of industrial life. Appealing to dissatisfaction and insecuri-

ties around the job, certain advertisements not only
offered their products as a kind of job insurance, but
intimated that through the use of their products one
might become a business success—the capitalist notion
of individual "self-"fulfillment.

Listerine, whose ads had taken the word *halitosis* out
of the inner reaches of the dictionary and placed it on
"stage, screen and in the home," offered this anecdote:

> He was conscious that something stood between him
> and greater business success—between him and
> greater popularity. Some subtle something he
> couldn't lay his hands on . . . Finally, one day, it
> dawned on him . . . the truth that his friends had
> been too delicate to mention.[71]

When a critical understanding of modern production might have helped many to understand what
actually stood "between them and greater business
success," this ad attempted to focus man's critique
against himself—his body had kept him from happiness. Within the world view of a society which was more
and more divorcing men from any notion of craft or
from any definable sort of product, it was also logical
that "you couldn't blame a man for firing an employee
with halitosis to hire one without it." The contingency of
a man's job was offered a nonviolent, apolitical solution.
If man was the victim of himself, the fruits of mass
production were his savior. Ads constantly hammered
away at everything that was his own—his bodily functions, his self-esteem—and offered something of theirs
as a socially more effective substitute.

In addition to the attempt on the part of advertising
to habituate people to buying as a solution to the
particular realities of a growing industrial society, ad
men presented products as means to what they viewed
as instinctual ends. Speaking often to women,[72] ads

offered daintiness, beauty, romance, grace, security and husbands through the use of certain products. Traditional advertising had conceived of these "ideals" as integrants of a Protestant notion of thrift and moderation. The dainty woman, a pillar of sense and temperance within the home, had been characterized as physically divorced from the marketplace, not to mention herself. Increasingly, within the texts of ads in the twenties, these desires are fulfilled in the marketplace. Thrift no longer cohabitates with daintiness, but threatens to prevent it. Within the rhetoric of these ads, the accumulation of various products, each for a separate objectified portion of the body, was equated with the means to success. Correlative to Allport's vision of "social self," advertising offered the next best thing—*a commodity self*—to people who were unhappy or could be convinced that they were unhappy about their lives. Each portion of the body was to be viewed critically, as a *potential* bauble in a successful assemblage. Woodbury's soap was offered as a perfect treatment for the "newly important face of Smart Today;" another product promised to keep teeth white: "A flashing smile is worth more than a good sized bank account. It wins friends." After she has used Caro Cocoanut Oil Shampoo, a dashing gentleman informs the lady, "I'm crazy about your hair. *It's* the most beautiful of any here tonight." Within the vision offered by such ads, not only were social grace and success attainable: they were also defined through the use of specific products. You don't make friends, your smile "wins" them; your embellished hair, and not you, is beautiful. "Smart Today" required one to compete on a social marketplace, though whatever was defined as smart would be gone tomorrow, yielding its momentary, though cataclysmic importance to a newly profitable "Smart Today." As the ads intimated that anything natural about the consumer was worthless or deplorable, and tried to make him schizophrenically self-conscious of that notion, they offered weapons by which even people with bad breath, enlarged nose pores, corned feet and other such maladies could eclipse themselves and "succeed."

As notions of failure were to be perceived within a style of self-denigrating paranoia, notions of success were likewise portrayed in purely self-involved terms. Though the victorious heroines of cosmetic advertisements always got their man, they did so out of a commodity defined *self-fetishization* which made that man and themselves almost irrelevant to the quality of their victory. Their romantic triumphs were ultimately commercially defined versions of the auto-erotic ones of Alban Berg's prostitute, *Lulu,* who declares that "When I looked at myself in the mirror I wished I were a man—a man married to me." (*"Als ich mich im Spiegel sah hatte ich ein Mann sein wollen . . . mein Mann."*)

During the twenties, civil society was increasingly characterized by mass industrial production. In an attempt to implicate men and women within the efficient process of production, advertising built a vision of culture which bound old notions of Civilization to the new realities of civil society. In what was viewed as their instinctual search for traditional ideals, people were offered a vision of civilized man which was transvaluated in terms of the pecuniary exigencies of society. Within a society that defined real life in terms of the monotonous insecurities of mass production, advertising attempted to create an alternative organization of life which would serve to channel man's desires for self, for social success, for leisure away from himself and his works, and toward a commoditized acceptance of "Civilization."

TWO
The Political Ideology of Consumption

Big business in America is producing what the Social-ists held up as their goal: food, shelter and clothing for all.

1 Assembling a New World of Facts

With the wide-scale implementation of mass production in the 1920s, advertising and the ideal of mass consumption were catapulted to the foreground of modern economic planning. In the internal arguments of the business community as well as in their more public expressions, American businessmen celebrated the coming of the new industrial age as one which would accelerate social progress among the masses and at the same time vindicate "the great stream of human selfishness" of which they were an undeniable part.[1] And yet the economic and social presence of a mass industrial machinery was not something that could arouse popular fidelity by virtue of its productive capacity alone. For as an increasingly large fraction of the material world became the domain of American business enterprise, the organization and manipulation of a responsive social context became clearly imperative. Faced on the one hand with the crisis of overproduction which prompted Bernard Baruch to issue the warning that while "we have learned to create wealth . . . we have not learned to keep that wealth from choking us,"[2] and on the other hand the emergence of tendencies and movements among the working classes which questioned the basis of capitalist wealth *per se*, businessmen sought to utilize their technology for their own political purposes. It became a central function of business to be able to define a social order which would feed and adhere to the demands of the productive process and at the same time absorb, neutralize and contain the transitional impulses of a working class emerging from the unrequited drudgery of nineteenth-century industrialization.

More and more, the language of business expressed the imperative of social and ideological hegemony. Such a development was not without its precedents in American history, or that of other nations, however. John Adams had spoken of the political requirements of industry. "Manufactures cannot live, much less thrive," he cautioned, "without honor, fidelity, punctuality, and private faith, a sacred respect for property, and the moral obligations of promises and contracts."[3] So too is much of American industrial development punctuated by attempts to channel thought and behavior into patterns which fitted the prescribed dimensions of industrial life.[4]

In a nineteenth-century society basically devoted to industrialization and regulating patterns of work, the arena of business manipulation was concerned predominantly with the basics of production. As Paul Nystrom, one of America's first consumer economists, wrote retrospectively of that early era: "under such conditions, society itself becomes industrialized. It develops its own ideals of life and puts its high stamp of approval on such virtues as working efficiency, special working ability, industry, thrift and sobriety. Respect and honor are paid to the principles of industrialism, and reverence is offered its founders and leaders. The captains of industry become popular heroes. These are the characteristics of a true industrial society, a society in which ideals of production rather than of consumption rule."[5]

With the development of methods of mass production and the expanded notion of markets that this entailed, the ideology of "private faith" to which John Adams had alluded became a matter that extended beyond the strictures of industry and of work. For the "new order" was one which sustained itself not merely around the question of labor fealty to the mechanical process of capitalism, but one which demanded a dedication of *all* social energy to a world being fashioned by industrial technology. It is out of such a modern imperative that Jacques Ellul, critic of technological society, has developed a common conception of *technology* and *technique* as a constellation of devices for the "technical management of physical and social worlds."[6]

By the 1920s businessmen had reached a considerable awareness of the political and social roles that the process of consumption and the advertising that stimulated it must play. Putting aside the buoyant ad rhetoric of progress and beneficence for a moment, *Printers' Ink* put the need for social control in the frankest terms: "modern machinery . . . made it not only possible but imperative that the masses should live lives of comfort and leisure; that the future of business lay in its ability to *manufacture customers* as well as products."[7] Elsewhere the business community was infused with a political messianism which implied that the mere selling of products was no longer an adequate goal of advertising. Writing in the twenties, Walter Pitkin, professor of marketing at the Columbia School of Journalism, spoke of goods advertising, even sophisticated "national" market goods advertising, as merely an initial step "in a direction toward which we must go a long way further." Even institutional advertising, a public relations scheme which tried to boost a whole sector of industry, did not meet the political demands of mass industrial society. What was necessary, rather, was a broad scaled strategy aimed at selling the way of life determined by a profit-seeking mass-productive machinery. Pitkin ordered a campaign for an entire industrial value system, imploring his colleagues "to go beyond institutional advertising to some new kind of philosophy of life advertising."[8]

Consumerism, the mass participation in the values of the mass-industrial market, thus emerged in the 1920s not as a smooth progression from earlier and less "developed" patterns of consumption, but rather as an aggressive device of corporate survival. Edward Filene, the Boston department store merchant and a man who had developed an international reputation as "the mouthpiece of industrial America,"[9] spoke frankly of the role and purpose of consumerizing the broad American population. The attempt to create a national, unified culture around the social bond of the consumer market was basically a project of broad "social planning."[10] Industry, Filene argued, could "sell to the masses all that it employs the masses to create," but such a development would require a selective education which limited the concept of social change and betterment to those commodified answers rolling off American conveyor belts. "Mass production demands the education of the masses," Filene axiomixed, "the masses must learn to behave like human beings in a mass production world."[11] Such an education, however, was to be one with extremely proscribed horizons. Fearing the implications of the kind of education that might suggest an adversary relationship between the interests of American workers and those of the captains of industry, Filene presented a vision of education into industrial and social democracy within which the element of conflict was eradicated from the world of *knowledge.* Education, for Filene, became a task of building a culture on the basis of "fact-finding." Just looking at the given "facts" about what is being produced rather than questioning the social bases upon which those facts lay was what modern education should be all about. Education should be a process of acclimating and adjusting the population to that world of *facts,* to make it their own. "The schools do their best to teach patriotism—loyalty to the political state . . ." Filene observed, "But what are the schools doing to interpret the machine civilization" to the citizenry?[12] "The time has come," he argued, "when all our educational institutions . . . must concentrate on the great social task of teaching the masses not what to think but *how to think,* and thus to find out how to behave like human beings in the machine age."[13] (My emphasis.)

The concept of "facts" as the essential world to which a worker should address him or herself is something that bore implications beyond the process of consumption. Although Filene's notion of *fact* was largely circumscribed by the wares of the commodity market, the notion of workers feeling comfortable in a world of fact reflects basic transformations in industrial life that characterize machine production and mass production in particular. As long as the apprentice-craftsman system had endured, earning a living was comprised of both productive activity and the social relations of commerce. Goods were made and sold for individuals, and the relationship between craftsmen and individual purchasers essentially affected the definition of work. In a highly mechanized machine production, however, where both commercial interchange and the interchange of long-term training had been eradicated, human intercourse had been largely excised from the work routine of laboring classes. Robert and Helen Lynd, in *Middletown*, their 1924 study of Muncie, Indiana, described how the world of people and the world of things had been cleaved from each other in the industrial process:

> Members of the [working class] . . . address their activities in getting their living primarily to *things*, utilizing material tools in the making of things and the performance of services, while members of [the business class] . . . address their activities predominantly to *people* in the selling or promotion of things, services, and ideas.[14]

Presenting "education" as an indoctrination into the world of facts of the marketplace—as opposed to the social relations of production and distribution—was a replication of developments which had shaped patterns of production. Consumption was but a reinforcement of the basic transformation that had increasingly characterized the world of work—a response to *things* rather than *people*, this time extended into daily life and leisure.

Widespread within the socially oriented literature of business in the twenties and thirties is a notion of educating people into an acceptance of the products and aesthetics of a mass-produced culture. Industrial development, then, became far more than a technological process, but also a process of organizing and controlling "long pent-up human impulses" (Filene) in such a way that these impulses might serve to provide social underpinnings to the industrial system.[15] Branding all patterns of life which resisted the domination of culture by the industrial machinery as "puritanism in consumption," Leverett S. Lyon's 1920s contribution to the *Encyclopedia of the Social Sciences* called for a training in industrial aesthetics to combat traditional patterns of culture. "What is most needed for American consumption," he wrote, "is training in art and taste in a generous consumption of goods, if such there can be. Advertising," he continued, "is the greatest force at work against the traditional economy of an age-long poverty as well as that of our own pioneer period; it is almost the only force at work against puritanism in consumption. It can infuse art into the things of life; and it will [!] . . ."[16]

Yet the argument for "education" that became so frequently heard among businessmen in the 1920s, and grew quite frantic as economic crisis appeared at hand,[17] was one which confronted many varieties of historical resistance. First of all, while the adoption of a consumerized mentality among working people might effect a political loyalty to the capitalistic premises of the industrial system, there was too little materially—during the 1920s—to secure such loyalties. Despite rhetorical calls among business people for "higher wages" as a tactic of social integration, wages among the vast number of working people remained too low and the desire for expanding profits among business too high to create a high level of material participation by workers in the commodity market.

During the 1920s, notes historian Irving Bernstein, wage earners "did not enjoy as great a rise in income as did those in higher brackets."[18] Citing figures worked out in Paul Douglas' 1924 study of "Wages and the Family," Bernstein argues that a majority of American working-class families throughout the twenties failed to earn a living which would make them consumers of any

great amount of goods beyond subsistence.[19] If an
"American" standard of consumption required at least
$2,000 to $2,400 annual income, as Douglas argued,
most wage-earning families (16,354,000 families according to Bernstein's calculations) received less than
$2,000 per year. While mass consumption rose steadily
throughout the twenties, it did not significantly alter the
amount of capital in-flow from working-class sectors of
the population. Where consumption rose among workers, it rose largely as a result of installment buying
on the one hand (this was also an aspect of middle-class consumption) or the forgoing of one set of goods
for another. Regarding the latter, the Lynd's study,
Middletown, indicates that the widespread consumption
of automobiles during the twenties, even among
working-class families, was often done at the expense of
clothing, food or the mortgaging of family property,
where it existed.[20]

Beyond this and perhaps more important to the
consciousness of many, were the indigenous networks
of social structure that carried premises and values
which generated mistrust or open opposition to the
corporate monopolization of culture. Traditional family
structures, agricultural life styles, immigrant values
which accounted for a vast percentage of the attitudes
of American working classes, and the traditional realms
of aesthetic expression—all these were historically infused with an agglomeration of self-sufficiency, communitarianism, localized popular culture, thrift and
subjective social bonds and experiences that stood, like
Indians, on the frontiers of industrial-cultural development. It was these subjective experiences of traditional
culture that stood between advancing industrial machinery and the synthesis of a new order of industrial
culture. And it was incumbent on industry, in formaliz-

ing the new order, to find a means to sacrifice the old. It was within this historical circumstance that the creation of an industrialized *education* into culture took on its political coloration.

Throughout the 1920s and 1930s the contiguity of industrialization and social control came to the fore in the United States and elsewhere. As Max Horkheimer, a social critic from the Frankfurt School, has noted in discussing monopolizing industrialism: "the rule of economy over all personal relationships, the universal control of commodities over the totality of life" must in the face of historical resistance become "a new and naked form of command and obedience."[21] Much as in the case of totalitarian Nazi Germany which he was addressing himself to, the advance of corporate industrialism required that "the objects of organization [be] . . . disorganized as subjects."[22]

2 Commercializing Expression

     In the propagation of an aesthetic of mass industrialism, it was in the realm of artistic creativity itself that the organization of objects and the dissolution of the subject took perhaps its most obvious toll. The business of advertising and marketing was one which drew heavily on creative human resources in order to formulate its product. The utilization of art in business promotion, wrote Walter Dill Scott, must maintain the primacy of profits. "To substitute the standard of the artist for the standard of the capitalist would be impossible in business," he noted decisively. Yet, understanding the ways in which the further use of the aesthetic dimension might enhance the social viability of capitalist mass production and distribution, Scott added that "a harmonious working of the two is [nonetheless] . . . possible."[23]

     Not coincidentally, the enormous growth of the advertising industry and the commercialization of art that it entailed took place along with the gradual depletion and demise of traditional sources and arenas of artistic expression and localized cultures. Artistic patronage, a province of the wealthy since ancient times, now was doled out through the economic avenues provided by advertising and its related industries (packaging for example). The effect on the graphic, literary and performing arts in America was to be monumental.

Newspapers, which throughout the nineteenth century had provided an arena for literary serialization and popular expression and whose diversity had provided for varied audiences, became increasingly commercialized and centralized in their direction. From 1900 through 1930 the number of daily newspapers in America declined steadily if not monumentally.[24] More important, there was an even greater decline in the existence of a diverse press. In 1909–10, 58 percent of American cities had a press that was varied both in ownership and perspective. By 1920, the same percentage represented those cities in which the press was controlled by an information monopoly. By 1930, 80 percent of American cities had given way to a press monopoly.[25] The role and influence of advertising in all of these developments is marked. In the period 1900–1930, national advertising revenues multiplied thirteen fold (from $200 million to $2.6 billion), and it was the periodicals, both the dailies and others, which acted as a major vehicle for this growth.

The immigrant press was particularly hard hit by commercial pressures. While the diversity of immigrant communities in America would have appeared to make the foreign language press an exception to the monopolistic development of American culture, that was hardly the case. In fact, it was within this press that some of the most naked forms of commercial control were exercised.

The American Association of Foreign Language Newspapers, under the direction of Louis N. Hammerling, was an advertising agency which catered specifically to the immigrant press. The association, formed by a back-room consortium of such corporations as Standard Oil, Consolidated Gas, American Tobacco Company and some members of the Republican National Committee, had first recruited Hammerling in 1909 out of the Wilkes-Barre lumber industry, where he had been an immigrant worker, to run the Republican campaign in the foreign language press.[26] As the head of the advertising association, Hammerling provided ads (both political and consumer) for most of America's non-English-language newspapers, and exerted a vast control over their political and economic orientation. Robert Park, a contemporaneous student of foreign-born communities in America, noted that Hammerling "could give advertising or he could take it away. He could promise the struggling little publisher that he would either make him or break him."[27] Frank Zotti, editor of *Narodni List,* described Hammerling's policy as one which was aimed to "secure patronage of large corporations, and through that patronage to subdue or at least control these smaller newspapers that were barely making an existence; and eventually to put Mr. Hammerling in the position of dictator to the foreign-language press."[28]

Hammerling did not merely feed ads to the non-English American press. Senate investigations into Hammerling's activities revealed that he also fed editorials and news material to these papers and required that they be published without the remuneration usually paid for advertising. Functioning as a "press bureau," the American Association of Foreign Language Newspapers was able to forge a political and social direction which was tantamount to almost total corporate control.[29]

Even after Hammerling was discredited in 1919 for forcing his clients to sign a pro-German "Appeal to Americans" in the early days of World War I and ousted from his position in the Association, the agency maintained its dedication to corporate development and the "Americanization" of immigrants. Under Hammerling's successor, Frances Alice Kellor, the association continued to equate the acceptance of American products with patriotism. Striking out for the destruction of all cultural distinctions within the nation, and dedicated to producing "one people in ideals"[30] through the unification of "racial and native born thought in this country,"[31] Kellor offered the commodity market as a bond which would insure that "the American point of view will prevail."[32]

Writing about the foreign language press in America as "an American institution, an American Advertising Medium, an Americanization Agency," Kellor offered a program for political consolidation:

> National advertising is the great Americanizer.
> American ideals and institutions, law, order and prosperity, have not yet been sold to all of our immigrants.
> American products and standards of living have not yet been bought by the foreign born in America . . .
> If Americans want to combine business and patriotism, they should advertise products, industry and American institutions in the American Foreign-Language press.[33]

Such a policy, argued Kellor, was crucial in order to combat heritages and behavior that were "so different from our own" as to constitute a threat of "action that is inimical to our national purposes, or that interferes with our social machinery."[34]

This centralization of control in the immigrant press is filled with political implications, but for now let it suffice to say that advertising in this press was of no small significance. By 1914, *Printers' Ink* noted that "foreign advertising is now about 20% of all the advertising in newspapers, and is constantly increasing."[35] By 1919, at his own admission,[36] Hammerling was a conduit for 5 percent of the entire national advertising revenues in the United States (around $145 million) and exerted commensurate economic influence in over 700 newspapers throughout the country.[37] Beyond Hammerling's operation, the centralization and commercialization of control was a phenomenon that spanned the widest range of publications, and the long-term effect of such a development on what kinds of creativity received publication and support has undoubtedly left a significant mark on American intellectual and cultural development in the twentieth century.

The relationship that developed between advertising and the whole question of artistic creativity was fundamentally connected to the broader process of consumerization. While advertising attempted to turn people away from traditional life-styles, within the confines of the ad industry itself, the sacrifice of creativity to the authority of commerce was also taking place. The proliferation of artists and writers employed in the ad industry was marked, as was the psychological attrition that they experienced in this association.[38] Artists, often gifted in their sensitivities and sympathies to human frailties, were called upon to use those sensitivities for manipulation. The result may be seen in the bitter renunciation of modern commerce that marks the writings of ex-ad men Sherwood Anderson, Wallace Stevens, and James Rorty (poet, and later editor of New Masses). All three, in their noncommercial writings, indicate the sense of artistic strangulation that capitalistic "patronage" of the arts had produced. Anderson's decrying of commerce as a system which has effected a "dreadful decay of taste, the separation of men from the sense of tools and materials"[39] is only echoed by Rorty's romanticized denunciation of commerce as a world which "is fueled by the organic cultural life which it disintegrates and consumes, but does not restore or replace."[40] While such flailings tend to glamorize preindustrial workmanship, they are nonetheless statements of anguish felt by the artist whose art has been conscripted and deformed.

This crisis in the arts, the emergence of advertising and the commercial mentality as a growing and increasingly exclusive arena for artistic endeavor, was a theme among writers who were not involved in advertising per se, but who nevertheless felt the demands of industry closing in on them, forging their profession. Based on real characters, Theodore Dreiser's novel, The Genius, dealt with the destruction of a painter (artist Eugene Witla) who found his "success" in the world of advertising as early as 1909. The commercialization of creativity may be found as a theme in the writings of Dos Passos, Randolph Bourne, Gertrude Stein and others. One of the most intense denunciations of the effect of commerce on intellectual life is James Agee's in the opening chapter of his study of southern sharecroppers, Let Us Now Praise Famous Men. While ending up with a defense of elite culture against an overcommercialized one, Agee too strikes to the heart of the crisis in creativity:

. . . the weak in courage are strong in cunning; and one by one, you have absorbed and have captured and dishonored, and have distilled of your deliverers the most ruinous of all your poisons; people hear Beethoven in concert halls or over a bridge game or to relax; Cézannes are hung on walls, reproduced, in natural wood frames; van Gogh is the man who cut off his ear and whose yellows became recently popular in window decoration; Swift loved individuals but hated the human race; Kafka is a fad; Blake is in the Modern Library; Freud is a Modern Library Giant; Dovschenko's *Frontier* is disliked by those who demand that it fit the Eisenstein esthetic; *nobody* reads *Joyce* any more; Céline is a madman who has incurred the hearty dislike of Alfred Kazin, reviewer for the *New York Herald Tribune* book section, and is, moreover, a fascist; I hope I need not mention Jesus Christ, of whom you have managed to make a dirty gentile.[41]

Fearing the fate of all artistic endeavor in the modern world, Agee pleads for his book. "Above all else: in God's name don't think of it as Art."

For many, the conscription of the arts by the industrial machine was a personal crisis. But perhaps more importantly, it represented a broad cultural tendency that was central to the ideology of consumerism—the eradication of indigenous cultural expression and the elevation of the consumer marketplace to the realm of an encompassing "Truth."

3 Advertising's *Truth*

The elevation of the goods and values of mass production to the realm of a *truth* was a primary task among those who sought to educate the masses to the logic of consumerism. Walter Pitkin's desire to create, through advertising, a *philosophy of life*[42] as well as Edward Filene's attempt to characterize the consumer market as *the* world of *facts*[43] are but representative examples of the process which Jung termed the transvaluation of the "word" into a system of "credulity."[44] This attempt to turn modern marketplace precepts into a "universal validity" (Jung) was, especially in the face of traditional cultural attitudes and patterns of consumption, central to the stability and survival of modern industrial capitalism.

Thus the elevation of advertising was significant not so much in terms of what it accepted and defined as reality but more in what it excluded from its reified conception of the world. Max Horkheimer, in his essay "The End of Reason" (1941), argued that the presentation of modern industrial society as *the world of facts* played a role which turned people away from their own needs, their ability to speculate on the solution of these needs, and ultimately from the notion of self-determination as a *democratic* principle. Appearing to be answering Filene's invocation of "fact-finding" directly, Horkheimer evaluated such principles:

> Today man needs factual knowledge, the automaton ability to react correctly, but he does not need that quiet consideration of diverse possibilities which presupposes the freedom and leisure of choice. . . . In the monopolistic apparatus none possesses that time and range.[45]

Elsewhere, this attack on the gerrymandered reality of industrial capitalism was equally vociferous. In 1921, Hungarian social critic Georg Lukács described this process of reification in telling detail, and here too (as will be demonstrated) the critique seems to answer directly the ideologues of mass consumerism. Writing in *History and Class Consciousness* (1921), Lukács described the obfuscation of social relations by the world of "facts" as follows:

> The essence of commodity-structure . . . is that a relation between people takes on the character of a thing and thus takes on a "phantom objectivity," an autonomy that seems so strictly rational and all-embracing as to conceal every trace of its fundamental nature: the relation between people.[46]

The thought of American businessmen themselves gave substance to the arguments of the critics that *Truth* and social control were largely interconnected. Within the schema of the businessmen the very notion of truth emanated not from any social values or ethics external to their business, but was a product of their business. As such, it is not at all surprising that the Progressive era's truth in advertising legislation, enacted in various states in the years following 1910, was not a move by irate citizens to clean up the ad business, but part of a public relations campaign which attempted to legitimize the ad industry's own conception of honesty. Paul Nystrom, the consumer economist, noted approvingly in 1929 that "the movement in the United States for truth in advertising has been sponsored by and promoted largely through advertising men. The International Advertising Association has for years carried on an intensive campaign to eliminate untruthful advertising, as have many local advertising groups. For many years the periodical *Printers' Ink* Weekly has carried on through its columns a promotion of a model statute to secure the elimination of untruthful advertising. The *Printers' Ink* statute has been passed by several of the state legislatures in the United States."[47]

The truth is that the *Printers' Ink* statute was rather soft and had few teeth in it. While making unlawful and punishable as a misdemeanor any ad which "contains any assertion, representation or statement of fact which is untrue, deceptive or misleading," the law was in no way armed to confront the problem of psychological manipulation; nor was it meant to.[48] Daniel Pope, in his unpublished dissertation, *The Development of National Advertising*, has expounded on the ways in which *Printers' Ink* developed a long-term struggle to circumvent the problems raised by consumers over such shucks as patent medicine.[49] Back into the nineteenth century, the magazine's concern with "truth" had been circuitous, and the self-regulation imposed by their model statute was, at best, minimal.

Yet, even as business was legislating itself into legitimacy, the campaign belied itself as but one more *sell*. In 1924, as the Associated Advertising Clubs of the World convened its annual convention in Great Britain, it revealingly adopted "Truth in Advertising" as its slogan and a "female form which," according to one participant, "was but scantily clothed in the shining garment of Truth" as its symbolic logos.[50] James Rorty attributed the following axiom to a former colleague: "Always tell the truth. Tell a lot of the truth. Tell a lot more of the truth than anybody expects you to tell. Never tell the whole truth."[51]

Purportedly a device of consumer protection, the installation of truth into advertising's ideological pantheon was one more form of attempted domination—not unfamiliar to students of the "big lie" which was emerging as a political tool elsewhere during these years. Not only was truth to be a guiding principle, but it also was an appeal within the ads themselves. "Gimbels Tells the Whole Truth" began one ad for the New York department store. Then, as if in quick response to the raised eyebrow of a skeptical and undoubtedly experienced reader, the ad attempted to cover up for past transgressions. "For years on end, we at Gimbels have been thinking that we were telling the Truth. . . . But what we have been telling was, so to speak, 'commercial truth!' We would tell you, quite honestly, that a certain pair of curtains had been copied, in design, from a famous model, that the colors were pleasing, that the price was very low. Every word of this was scrupulously true. But we may have failed to say that the curtains would probably fade after one or two seasons of wear."[52] Thus, Gimbels' copywriter provided a context within which the store and the reader shared a common ground—a basic distrust of "commercial truth."

While advertising's claim to the truth may have been shaky, it was this commitment to forging a consumer consciousness based on the "facts" of the marketplace that made ad men assume that the world of the ads would eventually become the common idiom of popular expression. George Phelps, whose advertising firm handled the big Detroit automotive accounts of the twenties, spoke aggressively of how advertising would increasingly define the accepted cultural idiom. "Advertising is a sharp and swiftly acting tool of business, and the only one by which a lone individual can engrave his message on the minds of the masses." Presenting the media as the "cannons" in this business offensive, he argued that modern technology provided a capability to relay information in such a way as to surpass traditional culture in its ability to influence behavior. The media, he contended, "have the capacity to multiply or broadcast impressions, to bombard the public with facts and ideas, to stimulate to action."[53] Through the use of media an image was projected in which people saw themselves held together, solving their life's problems through the benefit of commodities. Forerunners of modern TV ads, films of between one and five reels showing dramas in which given products played the heroic role, were produced by the ad industry. *Blow-out Bill's Busted Romance*, an advertising comedy, portrayed a particular brand of tires as the solution to the insecurities of love. Other films, such as *Sole-Mates*, a shoe comedy; *Candy Courtship* (for Lowney Candy Co.); and *Brushing the Clouds Away* (Fuller Brush), were produced in 1920 and 1921. Here, mass-produced commodities were located securely in daily life and shown to captive audiences in movie theaters along with the regular features.[54]

These attempts to alter the popular idioms of communication and "stimulate" behavior were clearly tied to a widespread program to shape a culture which responded to and communicated through advertising. As people increasingly took on the lingo of advertising, so too would basic social intercourse assume the role of stimulating consumption. In a rare articulation of the ad man's version of the utopian future, Robert Updegraff, writing in the magazine *Advertising and Selling*, postulated the "promise of the next quarter-century":

> . . . having learned the value of advertising as a commercial expression . . ., the world will next turn to advertising to make itself articulate in a broad social way. By 1950 men will have learned to express their ideas, their motives, their experiences, their hopes and ambitions as human beings, and their desires and aspirations as groups, by means of printed or painted advertising, or of messages projected through the air.[55]

Another ad man postulated that in the future "advertising will be attentively studied by the public: and will be read for its own sake."[56]

Phelps, the automobile advertiser, presented an elaborate fantasy of how people around the world would follow and trust the paternalistic suggestions of commercial propaganda:

> In luxurious metropolitan apartments and in the better thatched huts on the banks of the Congo River, people will hear from the lips of the president of Tomorrow's Transportation [a fictitious corporation] the description of its new world-wide air travel service and they will see him as he talks. . . . Furthermore, they will be glad to "listen and look in," for they have

learned from experience that the great international broadcasting organization does not make "straight broadcasts" as these plain business announcements without garnishing of entertainment are called, unless they are of broad social importance and promise to be of interest to the international millions. Not that the native of the valley of the Congo, or the native in his chalet in the Swiss Alps recognizes their social importance—he and his wife only know that they find them interesting. . . . They will read of this service in the advertising pages of their local periodicals. They will encounter it in various other media of advertising. When they do they will say to themselves, That is what that man with the kindly face told us about that night on the radio [sic] and they will have a feeling of friendliness toward Tomorrow's Transportation, Inc.[57]

Phelps' future was one in which commercial propaganda—elevated to the level of the only truth available—had infested the entire atmosphere. Within such a vision of the future, the notion of truth was "of interest" to the "citizens of industry," who were not expected to recognize or to particularly care about what was of social importance for them. Only the "great international broadcasting organization" was to determine what was important and what was not. Horkheimer's notion of *information* as discrete from the "consideration of diverse possibilities" finds documentation and fruition in the social framework of advertising's self-proclaimed future.

So, too, the relationship between the mass and "that man with the kindly face" is divested of any locus within the exchange process or the social relations that encompass it. Borne out is Lukács' critique of "phantom objectivity," a presentation of the world which obfuscates the fundamental relations of that world. In presenting a completely authoritarian vision of corporate domination, Phelps adopted a tone which clothed that authority in the garb of patriarchal wisdom. The conception of the future was one in which conflicts between people's needs and corporate development did not occur. Rather, the subjects of industry, be they the inhabitants of "luxurious metropolitan apartments" or the *natives* of the Congo, would passively and happily accept the rule of corporate judgment.

4 Obliterating the Factory

Loss of skills, the deification of the time-clock, the eradication of the work patterns of pre-industrial life, and the abomination of hazardous conditions around the machine—these had been both the characteristics of modern production and the fuel of widespread anticapitalist feeling among those who worked in the factories. Advertising's selective version of *Truth* was being formulated in order to bring about a widespread social dependency on the wares of mass production. Yet the immediate connection with industry that many experienced was the monotony of line production and/or the unsafe and poorly lit factory environment. Such work and working conditions were inextricably bound up in both the intensification of production and in much of the labor unrest that characterized industrialization throughout the evolution of the American factory system.

Throughout the nineteenth century, when the labor

77

force was conceived of as bound up mainly in production, it was felt that any failure on the part of the worker to assimilate the values of production was to be dealt with summarily. In 1869, *Scientific American,* a journal which identified with the science of production, spoke ominously of the fate in store for noncooperating immigrant laborers, promising them "a quiet but sure extermination."[58] In a more ideological vein, the Richmond, Virginia, *Whig* called for a broad educational program in industrial diligence. "[In] educating the industrial morale of the people . . . the work of inculcating industrial ideas and impulses, all proper agencies should be enlisted—family discipline, public school education, pulpit instruction, business standards and requirements, and the power and influence of the workingmen's associations."[59]

By the 1920s, however, industry was aware that the austerity of factory life which most workers experienced undermined the attempt to create a widespread consciousness of industrial commodities as forming an affirmative and indulgent culture. Within business thinking, then, it appeared necessary to eradicate the productive process from the ideology that surrounded the products. In ads, the commodities of industrial society were presented as means of circumventing the ills of industrial life. The reality of life within the factory only tended to cast aspersions on the visions of happiness projected in consumer ideology, and it was an essential principle of commercial propaganda that depiction of this reality be avoided at all costs.

Edward Filene attempted to paint an ecstatic picture of mass-production work. Adopting an authoritative tone, he exalted the democratic joys of monotonous labor. "It is a common mistake," he contended, "to assume that monotonous repetitive work is necessarily offensive. . . . Engineers have found, on the contrary, that most workers prefer to perform a simple, specialized, repetitive operation. It leaves their minds free to ruminate on other things. They do not abhor monotony, but desire it. . . ." For Filene, such an evaluation of human desires led to a connection between the "benefits" of monotony and the industrial aesthetic. This mass productive machinery "enables the unskilled, unintelligent man to earn more money than before with far less effort and with no harm to his mind and soul. It permits him to have an avocation as well as a vocation. . . . [It] puts the beautiful things it produces within the reach of the masses, and by creating an appreciation for beauty, where it did not exist before, makes the world a much better place to live in. . . . Beauty is the greatest objective of the world."[60]

Few other businessmen felt that an effort like Filene's to integrate an affirmative vision of work with an affirmative vision of the "spiritual truths" of consumer culture could possibly be successful. For the most part among the advertising and public relations elements of business, the success of consumerization depended on the ability to obfuscate the work process, to create an understanding of the industrial world which avoided any problematic reference to production altogether. Paul Nystrom, writing on the economics of fashion, noted that as wealth or social status were the basic selling points of most garments, "the styles should go as far as possible in proving that the owner does not have to work for a living."[61] What Thorstein Veblen had theorized as the conspicuous consumption habits of the leisure class were now propagated as a democratic ideal within mass advertising. In order to sell the commodity culture, it was necessary to confront people with a vision of that culture from which the class bases of dissatisfaction had been removed. Mark O'Dea, a leading New York advertising executive, wrote that the key to successful advertising copy was the ability to "release people from the limitations of their own lives."[62] If these limitations lay within the realm of the industrial process itself, it became all the more important to eradicate factory life as a constituent of visible culture within the ads. Essential to the growing sophistication of advertising technique, *Printers' Ink* noted retrospectively in 1938, was the move away from the objective conditions of the product:

> The first advertising told the name of the product. In the second stage, the specifications of the product were outlined. Then came emphasis upon the uses of the product. With each step the advertisement moved farther away from the factory viewpoint and edged itself closer into the mental processes of the consumer.[63]

Throughout advertising manuals, advertising which made mention of factory life is cited as "bad copy," deleterious to sales. Rather than locate products within an environment with which people had unhappy familiarity, it was argued that products should be placed in an environment tailored both to the psychological processes of the potential consumer and the economic priorities of the corporation. Helen Woodward, the leading woman copywriter of the 1920s, added that in order to write effective copy, the writer should avoid the productive arena religiously. "If you are advertising any product," she warned, "never see the factory in which it was made. . . . Don't watch the people at work. . . . Because, you see, when you know the truth about anything, the real, inner truth—it is very hard to write the surface fluff which sells it."[64]

5 Consumption and Social Change

With the development of an apparatus for the stimulation and creation of mass consumption, business assumed an expansionist and manipulative approach to the problem of popular consciousness. While much of the thinking in the American industrial "war rooms" maintained an adherence to traditional "democratic" rhetoric, the basic impulse in advertising was one of control, of actively channeling social impulses toward a support of corporation capitalism and its productive and distributive priorities. As the growth of American imperialism beyond our political borders had been couched in the Turnerian rhetoric of democracy on the one hand, and aggressive self-interest on the other, so too did the imperialization of the psyche (beyond the borders of production) take on a "trailblazing" aggressiveness toward the social frontiers which business hoped soon to civilize.

The corporate structure was the arena of production, and if the distribution of mass-produced commodities was to succeed, indigenous popular attitudes had to be supplanted where they tended to look elsewhere for the satisfaction of material and social needs. The conscription of social scientists like John B. Watson of Johns Hopkins into the ideological machinery represented the ascendency of such priorities. Watson, a founder of modern behavioral psychology, was a proponent of transferring psychological development away from the traditional arenas of socialization (e.g., the family) and for making the realities of commercial life the guiding principles of child-rearing. "We must face the fact that standards of training are changing," he declared, "and that these standards must now conform to the dominant trends in our changing civilization."[65]

Painting a sordid picture of traditional home life, one in which "unscrupulous nurses" were known to gratify infant wants by stroking, fondling and kissing their children, Watson contended that such nurturing was injurious to the individual and society.[66] Infantile sensual pleasure was, he felt, bad preparation for the social reality of commercial and professional life. Undercutting the home as an institution on which the child might rely, Watson led a move toward accepting the industrial apparatus as a more proper authority. "We have to stick to our jobs in commercial and professional life regardless of headaches, toothaches. . . . There is no one . . . to baby us." While the specific orientation of these pronouncements is geared toward encouraging a passive fidelity to the unsympathetic character of the workplace, Watson also provided psychological avenues by which home life might be supplanted by the stimulation of the senses—a direction toward which business in its advertising was increasingly gravitating. Pleasure that could be achieved by the individual within the home and community was attacked and deemphasized, as corporate enterprise formulated commoditized sensual gratification. Watson labeled all but the "gratifications" of the marketplace as perverse and psychologically and socially damaging. In 1922, he left Johns Hopkins to become a vice president of the J. Walter Thompson advertising agency, a place where his commercial proclivities were able to take on more practical forms.

Elsewhere, the call for a "new economic philosophy, a new business point of view, and . . . a new social system,"[67] was couched in aggressive and militaristic terms. The eradication of social attitudes which were resistant to consumption became a central concern among businessmen. The psychological conscription of consumers, said George Phelps, was simply a question of "influencing minds," or, more pointedly, "the process of getting people to do or think what you want them to do or think."[68] Viewing the potential consumer as a resource of industry, ad men spoke of the need to "reduce the principles of human action to a formula," adding that such was already integral to political manipulation outside of business.[69] Treating all people as mechanically identical, Edward Bernays, a nephew of Sigmund Freud and (along with Ivy Lee) a founder and leader of modern commercial public relations, called for the implementation of a "mass psychology" by which public opinion might be controlled.

> If we understand the mechanism and motives of the group mind, is it now possible to control and regiment the masses according to our will without their knowing it. . . .
> Mass psychology is as yet far from being an exact science and the mysteries of human motivation are by no means all revealed. But at least theory and practice have combined with sufficient success to permit us to

> know that in certain cases we can effect some change
> in public opinion . . . by operating a certain mecha-
> nism.[70]

Committed to the rhythms of the industrial machinery
and its economic priorities, the social psychologists
realized machinery as the all-informing idiom of social
life. The control of the masses required that people, like
the world they inhabited, assume the character of
machinery—predictable and without any aspirations
toward self-determination. As the industrial machinery
produced standardized goods, so did the psychology of
consumerization attempt to forge a notion of the "mass"
as "practically identical in all mental and social characteristics."[71]

The advertising media then had only to develop a
"science of unlocking the human mind."[72] The advertising of the future, declared George Phelps, will be
effective in so far as it is able to "leap to the eye . . . leap
to the mind."[73] All activity was envisioned as taking
place within the corporate walls; the prospects for the
consumer were no more than a passive (if "gratified")
spectatorship. The human eye became merely a target
for visual stimulation, the ear was but an "avenue of
entry" for the blandishments of advertising.[74]

And yet, if social passivity was a futuristic political
utopia projected by the philosophers of Madison Avenue, so too was it a reflection of the frustrated social
world which American industrialization was actually
creating.

Just as the factory was eradicated from the affirmative vision of productivity, so too was the propagation of
a utopian vision of passivity an attempt to neutralize the
frustrated passivity of daily life that, even in the ad-
missions of businessmen, increasingly characterized

industrial society. Industrial growth in America had institutionalized monotony as a feature of work and "disappointment with achievements" as a common malaise, noted business economist Paul Nystrom. It was the absence of any forceful social bonds and the development of a widespread "*philosophy of futility*," he continued, that might be effectively mobilized in the stimulation of consumption. Speaking of the seeming purposelessness of American industrial life itself, Nystrom noted that "this lack of purpose in life has an effect on consumption similar to that of having a narrow life interest, that is, in concentrating human attention on the more superficial things that comprise much of *fashionable* consumption." The mass-produced goods of the marketplace were conceived of as providing an ideology of "change" neutralized to the extent that it would be unable to effect significant alteration in the relationship between individuals and the corporate structure. "Fatigue" with the futility of modern life might, if all other avenues of change are eradicated, be channeled toward a "fatigue . . . with apparel and goods used in one's immediate surroundings."[75]

The conception of consumption as an alternative to other modes of change proliferates within business literature of the twenties. Given the recent history of anticapitalist sentiments and actions among the working class, the unpleasant possibility of "deeper changes" gave flight to a more pacified notion of social welfare that emanated from consumerization. Recognizing the irreversability of frustration among those who felt trapped in their surroundings, Helen Woodward spoke frankly of consumption as a sublimation of urges that might be dangerous in other form. Admitting that change would be "the most beneficent medicine in the world to most people," Woodward offered mass consumption as a means of acting out such impulses within a socially controllable context. "To those who cannot change their whole lives or occupations," she began, "even a new line in a dress is often a relief. The woman who is tired of her husband or her home or a job feels some lifting of the weight of life from seeing a straight line change into a bouffant, or a gray pass into beige." The basic issues of industrial capitalism were fractionalized, isolated and reduced to trivialities in her formula. "Most people," Woodward declared, "do not have the courage or the understanding to make deeper changes."[76]

The logic of using consumption and *mass* leisure as ameliorations for boredom and social entrapment was not merely an underlying trend in advertising. Some ads made explicit reference to the inadequacies of modern existence, and frankly offered the culture of modern industrialism as an *ersatz* for meaningful activity. Robert and Helen Lynd culled the following ad from the *Saturday Evening Post* in 1924; an advertisement for the motion picture industry, it lends some credence to Kafka's blanket indictment of the cinema as an art form which puts the eyes "in uniform":

> Go to a motion picture . . . and let yourself go. . . . Before you know it, you are living the story— laughing, loving, hating, struggling, winning! All the romance, all the excitement you lack in your daily life are—in Pictures. They take you completely out of yourself into a wonderful new world. . . . Out of the cage of everyday existence! If only for an afternoon or an evening—escape.[77]

Here meaningful activity is clearly divorced from the context of daily life. The ad speaks for the fantasy value of the cinema—placing the gratification of emotional needs squarely within the symbolic function of mechanically reproduced, spectatorial culture.

The ideologically politicized realm of consumption was clearly seen by industrial society as a device by which social change, the passing of "gray . . . into beige," might be symbolically acted out in the public culture. Through the creation of a spectacle of *change*, frustrations and boredom within the context of industrial society might be mobilized to maintain and sustain that order. Thus the political imperative of legitimizing industry and delegitimizing the individual and the immediate expressions of community as proper realms of authority would be achieved. To quote Denys Thompson, a contemporary English critic, "Advertising tries to conceal the emptiness and make life feel good. It is as if the forces of advertising had decreed that the individual man or woman must not be allowed to develop his or her own potentialities."[78]

Within the symbolic spectacle, the passivity and acceptance of the marketplace was shown to be more favorable for the consumer than other, more radical conceptions of change. "Mass production," contended merchant Edward Filene, "holds possibilities of accomplishing for mankind all of the good that theoretical reformers or irrational radicals hope to secure by revolutionary means."[79] "Business men will continue to oppose political revolutions, but not in the negative way in which they have opposed them in the past," noted Filene. Direct political repression as a policy had peaked a few years before with the "Red Scare," the Palmer raids, and the massive deportation of immigrant workers; now was the time for a more indirect and positive strategy. In the vacuum created in once explosive communities, business could afford to be sensitive to the fact that when "something wrong is happening" in people's lives, they must "direct their energies" toward meeting the roots of dissatisfaction.[80] But, Filene cautioned, in order to "live successfully in the Machine Age," we must rely on the facts of the modern marketplace and demand "the abandonment of all class thinking."[81]

Frances Kellor, the enlightened director of the American Association of Foreign Language Newspapers, spoke even more directly than Filene regarding the political role that advertising would have to play within the vast immigrant and first-generation American communities. "It is the answer to Bolshevism," she declared, a fundamental process of Americanization.[82] If business were unable to provide a commercialized notion of leisure, Paul Nystrom warned, then socialization appeared to be the "only practical substitute."[83]

The idea of mass consumption, or at least an ideology of mass consumption as a commercially viable answer to "class thinking," also found its way into the ads themselves. Goods, as presented in the ads, would provide a bond between groups of people who traditionally were at antagonistic ends of the political structure. In a promotion of one commodity after another, we see bosses treating well-sold workers as equals and firing those who have not bought effectively. Another tack, taken by the Parker Pen Company, appeared in an ad of the twenties. Perhaps proving, at least in its own commercial logic, that the pen is mightier than the sword in solving seemingly irreconcilable social differences, this ad for Parker was signed by the presidents of United States Steel and the Baltimore and Ohio Railroad on the one hand, and by labor leader Samuel Gompers and socialist author H. G. Wells, on the other. Where all else might tend to accentuate their differences, it was through the remarkable assent as to the quality of the Parker Pen that all was apparently resolved.

Integrating the mass consumption of goods into the negative political process of combatting bolshevism and "class" politics in general, consumerism also assumed a positive political character in the ideology of business. Within the political ideology of consumption, *democracy* emerged as a natural expression of American industrial production—if not a by-product of the commodity system. The equation of the consumption of goods with political freedom made such a configuration possible. Expounding on the notion of political democracy, Filene noted that within the expanding industrial context, "the masses must be taken into full citizenship. They must achieve, not mere literacy, but culture." The culture to which he referred was one based on the process of "fact-finding"—acquainting oneself with the variety of goods with which one might live in this "machine civilization."[84] For consumer economist Elizabeth Hoyt, a woman who shared the view of consumption as a democratizing process, the definition of this democratic *culture* was part of a task by which industry determined "for a people what they consider worth consuming."[85] Yet within each of these notions of political democracy, there was an implicit acceptance of the centralization of the political process. Democracy was never treated as something that flowed out of people's needs or desires, but was rather an expression of people's ability to participate in and emulate the "pluralism of values"[86] which were paraded before people and which filtered downward from the directors of business enterprise.

In the economics of consumerism, a field that emerged in the 1920s in the works of Elizabeth Hoyt, Hezel Kyrk, Paul Nystrom, *et al*, the notion of "marginal utility" came into being. Here, the notion of value is extended beyond the question of how a given commodity is to be *used* by people in their daily lives. The concept of "marginal utility" confronts the entry into the economic world of a notion of *value* which is politicized rather than concerned with direct application. Thus, "marginal utility" defines such economic elements as fashion, taste, status-giving function, suggestion of sensuality, a broad range of aesthetic values which apply to a product, and ultimately, the political implications of a commodity, a broad range of commodities, or of consumption itself.[87]

The essential marginal utility of the constellation of goods that defined the modern commodity market was located in a series of object-oriented life alternatives which were posed as a definition for the level of democracy to which American society had climbed. In so far as traditional "democratic institutions" such as the free press, popular education and representative government were of aid in familiarizing the population with the benefits of modern consumption, disaffected ad-man James Rorty pointed out, they too might be considered to achieve the level of democracy which characterized the advertising industry.[88] Education should encourage consumption and an adherence to the pluralism of commodities, noted economist Nystrom. "A democratic system of education," he added, ". . . is one of the surest ways of creating and greatly extending markets for goods of all kinds and especially those goods in which fashion ["marginal utility"] may play a part."[89]

This notion of democratic education was implemented as schools instituted "tooth-brush drills" at the instigation of companies which made toothbrushes. So too did science students see the various stages in the production of cocoa dramatized by models provided conspicuously by the leading producer of cocoa. Democratic education not only familiarized the young with processes but also with products.

Within all of these democratic pronouncements, the essential political impulse was one of entrepreneurial domination, a structure in which *political* choice was limited to the prescriptions formulated by business and *politicized* in its advertising. "The competition of ideas," as propagated in advertising and public relations, argued Edward Bernays, "is an essential democratic process, for then the public can make its own choice."

Even with such a self-protecting conception of democracy, however, there were some among the business community who were to adopt a clearly antidemocratic stance.[90] Fearing the democratic possibilities in the public at large, as well as the problem of governmental intervention and control over business, some businessmen cast continuous aspersions on the traditionally political realms of government and civil society. Such proponents of industrial democracy as Edward Filene suggested that even voting for what and for whom they want "the masses may or may not achieve political democracy."[91] As an alternative for this faulted political system, Filene argued that the process of consumption provided an effective arena for democratic participation. By buying the goods of large industries, and by participating in the economic solvency of these industrial giants, people were electing a government which would constantly be satisfying their needs and desires; the democratic process was becoming one which was turning the political realm away from its traditional governmental concerns and solidifying it within the economic processes of modern industrial capitalism. "It is within the structure of business," contended Filene, that "the wisest and best leadership is actually being chosen by the people." Consumerism was a process which not only sustained big business economically, but also sustained its ascendency politically. By buying, people were democratically legitimizing the dominant role that industrialists aspired to play in all levels of political life.

Giving substance to his contention that consumption was a political process, Filene announced the political ascendency of business and its productive priorities. Through consumption, he contended, "the masses of America have elected Henry Ford. They have elected General Motors. They have elected the General Electric Company, and Woolworth's and all the other great industrial and business leaders of the day."[92] By far more democratic than traditional representative government, consumption was not merely a process for people to elect "their industrial government" but was moreover a way of "constantly participating in it."[93] Participation in an industrially defined marketplace had become a modern expression of popular political activity, yet it was an activity that maintained American industrial barons as the social directors of the nation, for "participation" in no way implied control or determination. Mass production was, in Filene's words, "*production for the masses*" and however this production encroached on people's activities and proclivities was of little relevance to the new democracy that was being theorized for the emerging mass society.

As James Madison had defined the spread and variety of factions as a protection of liberty within the early republic, the political theorists of mass industrial America saw the competition of ideas on the consumer marketplace as a modern expression of liberty. While Madison's competition of factions had been designed to ensure that any given faction would not gain ascendency or effectively threaten vested interests, factional components of the modern political arena were already laundered of any dangerousness or subversion. Variegated expression was now found in the competition of "propagandas" that mass advertising and public relations created, ensuring liberty, as Edward Bernays argued, by the free exchange by "proponents and opponents of every propaganda" that defined the activity of the modern marketplace.[94]

Here, too, the notion of any form of popular direction or determination is neatly cleaved from the modern conception of democracy as businessmen defined it. Speaking of the impracticality of popular democracy, Bernays felt that representative government must now be delegated to the wisdom of industry, to the "industrial government" which had been canonized in Filene's political thought. Speaking for the nation, Bernays surrendered the realm of political judgment and the definition of the socially *possible* to the industrialists whom he had faithfully represented as a public relations man. "We have voluntarily agreed," he began, "to let an invisible government sift the data and high-spot the outstanding issues so that our field of choice shall be narrowed to practical proportions."[95] Within such a context, it is not surprising that *Scientific American*, already noted for its corporate sympathies, called for a restoration to respectability of that "fine old word *propaganda*." Decrying the totalitarian implications that *propaganda* had assumed, the journal lamented that "there is no word in the English language . . . whose meaning has been so sadly distorted."[96]

For Bernays, marketplace control over popular behavior became tantamount to a "Declaration of Independence" from less developed and more popular definitions of democracy. "The conscious and intelligent manipulation of the organized habits and opinions of the masses is an important element in a democratic society," he proclaimed. Speaking affirmatively and patriotically of the emergence of the vast media of corporate propaganda, Bernays placed the responsibility for defining the universe of political discourse in the hands of the anonymous inhabitants of Madison Avenue. "We are governed, our minds are molded, our tastes formed, our ideas suggested, largely by men we have never heard of. This is a logical result of the way in which our democratic society is organized."[97]

Freedom became increasingly characterized in authoritarian terms, and at times even the democratic rhetoric was dropped from business pronouncements regarding the desirability of corporate social control. One business theorist contended that freedom and equality could be translated into the ability of each person to emulate or aspire to emulate the tastes of the upper classes; "and what could be a better method of doing this [proving equality] than by consumption."[98] The "fashion cycle," he contended, was an expression of the tastes and values of the wealthy, yet through the mass production of low-priced goods which imitated "high-priced merchandise," upper-class values might be internalized within the culture of the poor. "Reproduction of high-priced goods into lower-priced goods makes it possible for people of lower incomes to participate in the fashion cycle."[99]

For those who might refrain from such participation, the society would provide its own grave consequences. Paul Nystrom warned:

> There will be quizzical looks, doubtful stares and critical estimates. He will be thought queer. He will be judged as lacking in brain power and, perhaps, as an undesirable person. If he persists [in violating the

norms of consumption] . . . he will, if he is an employee, lose his job! He will lose customers if he is a salesman; he will lose votes if he is a politician. He will lose his custom if he is a doctor or a lawyer. He will lose all of his friends.[100]

Within such a conception of social security, variation from the norms of consumption as defined by industry, whether in the name of some vague sense of individuality or in the name of the customs and habits of any group of people within the population, was tantamount to disaster. Traditional social bonds and the conformities that they engendered were un-American and suspect. The social bonds of the modern age, argued Nystrom, would be provided over-the-counter, and any other course would lead to "inevitable" ostracism, the loss of esteem and job security. Elizabeth Hoyt noted that most of the hostilities toward the various ethnic communities could be clearly connected to these people's violation of the norms of consumption. "I'd like them better if they didn't wear such queer clothes," Hoyt reported, quoting an alleged *American* housewife "of her foreign neighbors." Elsewhere, she observed, there were a variety of racial/ethnic epithets—"Frog-eating Frenchmen" and "Mackerel Snappers"—that spoke to the primacy of proper consumption habits among *Americans.* Accepting such a definition of *Americans* as those who comment on their *foreign* neighbors, Hoyt noted that there was but a hair's breadth of difference between the problem of "questionable consumption" and that of "questionable consumers."[101]

And so the American political tradition was being forged, in the minds of businessmen, along the patterns of proper and proscribed consumption. Reinforcing the authoritarian political function of a mass-produced marketplace, it was *Harper's Bazaar,* a dictator of the fashion industry's pronouncements, that commented on the political dilemma that consumption patterns posed for the population at large. Marking the end of true economic competition in the functional world of goods and heralding the distinction between libertarian rhetoric and the actualities of consumption, *Bazaar* noted the eclipse of freedom in the world of goods in a way which harkened to the eclipse of freedom in the world of politics:

> The pioneering hard-fisted, hard-boiled American Male will cheer campaign speeches on the benefits of rugged individualism and whistle laissez-faire, whenever he has to keep up his courage in a financial crisis. He will grow turgidly eloquent on the benefits both to himself and society of doing just what he sees fit when and if he pleases. He will battle to his last breath against any code prescribing a uniform way of running his business, auditing his accounts, educating his children or divorcing his wives. Any form of regulation is to him a symptom of Bolshevik tyranny. But the one moment when he is terrified of freedom is when he buys his clothes. *He is more afraid of wearing a bright orange necktie to his office than of carrying a red flag in a communist parade.* (My emphasis.)[102]

Democratic rhetoric or not, the formulators of the consumer market and the propagandists who publicized it hoped to instill an authoritarian obedience to the dictates of daily life in the machine age. Ad men attempted to convey a picture of the world in which small groups were no longer proper realms for the communication of values—it was within the corporation and the mass-industrial context that people might find a replacement for outdated communities and the sustenance they afforded. Men and women, prognosticated ad man Robert Updegraff, "must awaken to the futility of trying to express themselves in a handful way." Only within the context of "millions" does modern communication take place.[103] This sentiment was echoed by the leading spokeswoman of home economics, Christine Frederick. Herself a student of advertising—she had been a disciple of Walter Dill Scott at Northwestern—Frederick also inveighed against the attempt to communicate on the level of community. Talking to the issue of consumer protection, she belittled any efforts on the part of people to form their own movements. Such, she felt, was not the *stuff* of modern life. In terms of consumer protection, people had three places to look for help to assure proper quality control: the government, the big consumer groups (such as the Consumer Union—founded and directed by Edward Filene, no less), and the big testing labs and universities. The issue of *consumer protection* was too large to be actuated on the level of popular politics.[104]

While ads continually painted a picture in which people could trust no one (not even themselves) in their immediate surroundings, the corporations were presented as an alternative for communities which were pictured as being eroded by mistrust: people fragmented from one another by such privatized problems as "sneaker smell," "paralyzed pores," "vacation knees," "spoon-food face," "office hips," "underarm offense," and "ashtray breath." The immediate world of the "consumer" was in fact presented as one in which *fear* justifiably reigned. Quoting an AMA report in *Hygeia* magazine, early consumer advocate Stuart Chase noted that "for ordinary people" the basic function of mouthwashes and "their practical use, is confined to scaring us to death."[105] An advertisement for the Yale lock company showed a woman lying in bed, blissfully naïve, with the shadow of an approaching man shed ominously on her bedroom wall. The caption read as follows: "Night loneliness . . . the sound of stealthy tampering at the door . . . a moment of helpless terror. . . ." As would be expected, the Yale company made no call for better community and social relations, but omnipotently announced, "Yale Banishes Fear! from your home." An ad agency head informed copywriter Helen Woodward how to write an ad for baby food:

> Give 'em the figures about the baby death rate—but don't say it flatly. You know if you just put a lot of figures in front of a woman she passes you by. If we only had the nerve to put a hearse in the ad, you couldn't keep the women away from the food.[106]

One such ad did appear. Although there was no hearse, the illustration showed an ominously empty pair of baby shoes. Refining the notion of the effective use of *fear* in making sales, ad man George Burton Hotchkiss noted: "Fear in itself . . . is paralyzing; it robs one of the power of action. No one buys anything through fear, but rather through the instinct of self-preservation or some other reaction that is almost inseparable from fear."[107]

Morrill Goddard, editor of Hearst's *American* weekly and the man who *invented* the Sunday newspaper, wrote of *fear* as a basic appeal and, according to at least one major New York ad agency, greatly affected their strategy.[108] The head of that agency, Mark O'Dea, spoke of *fear* manipulation in heroic terms. Taking issue with Roosevelt's pronouncement in the early days of the Depression that "we have nothing to fear but fear itself," O'Dea presented a broad historical overview to vindicate *fear* manipulation as "our national salvation." It was, after all, he argued, the "fear of tyranny that drove our colonies into becoming a republic."[109] Expounding further on the beneficent role of fear in history, O'Dea penned this justification for commercial terror tactics:

> Since time began, Fear has been a regulatory part of humanity—our primitive religion taught the vengeance of the gods, our modern revivalists, like Billy Sunday, frightened people with damnation.
> Fear of mediocrity drove a little Corsican into becoming Emperor—Europe's fears drove Napoleon into exile. Fear made Patrick Henry a patriot. Fear stalked with Lincoln from his log cabin to his tomb. It was the spur of such men as Martin Luther, Poe, Peter the Great, Chopin, Julius Caesar, Balzac, John the Baptist.
> So what's a little Fear in advertising.[110]
>
> We've a better world with a bit of the proper kind of Fear in advertising . . . fear in women of being frumps, fear in men of being duds.[111]

Within the ads, as I have discussed elsewhere, this fear took on the character of presenting a world in which the individual was constantly judged by others, a world in which there was the total absence of positive bonds between people. The individualism which had been at the heart of liberal bourgeois thought throughout the preceding century and a half, had turned rancid, had become the core of uncertainty and social degeneration.

Yet in the midst of such a manipulated reality, there was one bastion of security, one area in which people were held together—the industrial corporation. By appealing to the emotions in its ads ("Make 'em weep" were one boss's instructions to an inexperienced copywriter), industry hoped not merely to sell goods, but also to capitalize on and conscript the basic emotional structures of people. Even as all else goes wrong, the ads asserted, the corporation will provide for you. Helen Woodward designed one ad showing "a man lying bandaged in a bed, smiling joyously as a postman came up and handed him a check from the Aetna company."[112] Here was the vision of a precarious social life (whether the man was the victim of an industrial accident is not indicated) ameliorated by a *concerned* corporation.

During the twenties, corporate advertising often worked to create a personified conception of its own beneficence. While daily life was projected as a flux of disastrous and unpredictable events, "image" advertising (often termed "good-will" advertising) studied methods of locating stability and reliability within the corporate walls. Claude Hopkins, a dominant figure in the advertising industry of the twenties, wrote in *Scientific Advertising* (1923), that as a contrast to the hostile and hazardous world portrayed in the ads, corporations must work to create a nurturing image of a permanence which would defy the upheavals of day to day existence: "We try to give each advertiser a becoming style. We make him distinctive, perhaps not in appearance, but in manner and tone. He is given an individuality best suited to the people he addresses. . . . That's why we have signed ads sometimes—to give them a personal authority. A man is talking—a man who takes pride in his accomplishments—not a soulless corporation!"[113]

As quality and craft were eliminated from the workplace, the corporations tried to create an image of themselves as a repository of craft to which people would gravitate. As president of Lord and Thomas Agency, which claimed (1923) to be the largest in the world, we can assume that within the advertising business itself, Hopkins was sensitive to the public relations requirements of a large corporation. As he spoke personally for his own large business, so too did he espouse "individuality" as a necessary public image. While the advertising public was expected to compulsively change and vary according to the dictates of the market, such fluctuations in a business were not, according to Hopkins, characteristics which would inspire public fealty. In forging a business image, he noted, "we take care not to change an individuality which has proved appealing. . . . In successful advertising, great pains are taken never to change our tone. . . . Appearing different every time we meet never builds up confidence."[114] Thus, the fluctuations in style, fashion and "progress" which characterized those who adhered to the whims of the commodity market might be assumed to undercut any level of mutual confidence, whereas the stable individuality of the corporation would prove increasingly attractive and trustworthy. In advertising campaigns, the image of the corporation was reinforced by such broad strategies. An ad for the telephone company, one which must be seen in the context of *fear* appeals about the immediate surroundings of the potential consumer, projects a rare vision of community and sustenance:

> The biggest thing about your telephone is the spirit of thousands and thousands of people who make up the Bell system. . . . The loyalty of these people to the ideals of their work is reflected in every phase of your telephone service.[115]

A 1928 ad for Maxwell House Coffee presented the product as but a canned version of "Joel Cheek's original blend," blended "patiently and skillfully."[116] The General Motors Corporation offered its own version of *hand-crafted, pre-industrial* quality in their "Bodies by

Fisher," still a trademark. In a 1928 ad for G.M., this artisan concept of quality was miraculously bound to the vast network of oligopoly: "Everywhere you go, note how the cars with Fisher Bodies stand out. . . . It is perfectly plain that the most beautiful cars in every price class are those with Bodies by Fisher . . . those cars whose bodies are the products of Fisher artistry, Fisher craftsmanship and Fisher's unrivaled resources."[117] Another ad for the Bell telephone system noted that talking through a phone conveyed "all the conviction of a human voice," creating a bond between you and the recipient of the call. In terms of "thought, mood, and personality," the telephone was the "road home."[118] At the same time that corporations portrayed their own social fabric with such sanguinity, it must be remembered, the ads which were directed at home life, community and the workplace reminded people that in case of social failure, "Suspect yourself first" (Listerine)!, and then move on to your wife, husband, neighbors, etc.[119]

In drafting an affirmative conception of human characteristics, the business community was setting up itself, or its personified corporate self, as a model for emulation. Ads and public relations portrayed the corporation as a function of social intercourse which created positive bonds where all else had failed. The authority of industry was being drawn as a sustaining *father* figure while the traditional arenas of social intercourse and the possibility of collective action were pictured as decrepit, threatening, and basically incapable of providing any level of security.

6 Consumption: A Partial Totality

     While many of the products of the marketplace were still financially and socially inaccessible to people, and where their accessibility required an increasing commitment to installment buying, still the ads portrayed the consumer market as an integrated and totalistic world view. Moreover, where resistance to the current direction and control of industry was manifest, it was ideologically severed from the vision of social experience proffered by the ads. The possibility of a world benefited by industrial technique yet respectful of popular determination and activity had been a central demand of working-class struggle for almost a century. Yet in *acceding* to the demand for industrial democracy, the machinery of corporate ideology had distilled out these critical questions. The ideologues of business, whose industry had altered the very process of industrial production, were cognizant of the need for wide-scale popular involvement in an expanding industrial culture. They responded by creating a cultural model by

103

which that involvement was one of acting out the prescribed social roles of corporate planning. Art would flourish, but it would flourish within the aesthetic realms of business. Economy would dictate the creative dimension of industrial America, and the arenas of expression—newspapers, magazines, media, schools of design, etc.—were thus circumscribed.

Immigrants would be Americanized, a process identical to an abolition of their common memories and the replacement of them by a "mass" perception keyed to the vaulted aspirations for mass-produced goods. The concept of truth would be limited to the truths surrounding American goods and would reflect an ethical persuasion which might be constantly "outgrown" so as to conform to the overriding "rules for profit making."[120]

In the futuristic dreams of the ad men of the twenties, there soon would be a world in which ads would provide a common idiom of expression; language and communication would take on the role of constant selling; and the ongoing discontent with things *as they are* would seek amelioration according to that idiom. Dream and reality became equated in the world of ideas generated by the marketplace. Where reality did not conform to the dream, the reality was reformed (ideologically) so as to imply a world in which people didn't work and an industrial apparatus which had no factories.

In *Mythologies*, an interesting study of 1950s French culture, Roland Barthes has noted that much of modern industrial design is such that it seems to defy familiar mechanics and "natural law." Speaking specifically of the Citroen DS (automobile), Barthes notes that we can see the "beginning of a new phenomenology of assembling." He explains: "[It] is as if one progressed from a world where elements are welded to a world where they are juxtaposed and hold together by sole virtue of their wondrous shape." This, he adds, "is meant to prepare one for the idea of a more benign Nature."[121] Benign, partly because the element of human tension has been excised from it; a conception of products which denies not only the reality of human participation in production, but also the ability of human understanding to comprehend their mystified Nature. Within such a world, the product takes on a mysterious reality impervious to the understanding or action of the population.

What Barthes describes as a "new phenomenology of assembling" was not new to the context of the 1950s. The mystification of the production process, the separation of people (both as producers and consumers) from an understanding of this process, may be seen emerging early in the twentieth century. Yet the mystification is not one which limits itself to hiding the mechanics behind a "wondrous shape." In the productive process itself, one of the characteristics of "scientific management" beyond and perhaps more important than its efficiency, is its separation of the work process from an understanding of what is being made. In the American steel industry, as early as 1910, the "routing" systems of production tended to make the workers' understanding of mechanical process anachronistic. Samuel Haber, a historian, has culled the following insight into "scientifically managed" industry created by Frederick Taylor:

> One of the most important general principles of Taylor's system was that the man who did the work could not derive or fully understand its science. The result was a radical separation of thinking from

doing. Those who understood were to plan the work and set the procedures; the workmen were simply to carry them into effect.[122]

A phenomenon of industrial capitalism, the "separation of thinking from doing," cut deeply into widespread labor demands for control over the work place. The demand for such control had come from a historical tradition. It had been based in a sense of self-defined workmanship as well as an experienced understanding of the contours of an environment fit to live and work in. As technical "know-how" became imposed upon the worker in the form of management from above, the self-perception of the worker as the source of productive knowledge was historically undercut. Industrial skill became located within the confines of industrial organization and management.

Whereas the first manifestations of this tendency took place on the shop floor, it quickly spread to the arenas of consumption. Many early twentieth-century consumer goods—the Model T is a good example—were products of mass industry, and yet still assumed a level of mechanical know-how and understanding on the part of the consumer. Ford's Model T was the consumer's to repair; it was a power plant which people could adapt to farm tasks or to generating electricity. So too with other home and professional equipment. One dentist interviewed has indicated that as late as 1938, when he entered practice, he had the responsibility of servicing and repairing his own equipment.

Yet by the 1920s both advertising and product design moved in the direction of separating products from the general knowledge of mechanics and from technical understanding—moving in the direction of aesthetic and linguistic mystification. The common development in usage of words such as *halitosis* and *acidosis* placed the burden of definition in corporate hands.

The Gillette Razor Company in its advertising of the mid-1920s announced a razor with a new dimension, a *slanted head*. The ad was crammed with all sorts of technical data and jargon, but it was a totally mystified technical idiom. *The Journal of Applied Psychology*, doing a follow-up on the ad, noted that while subjects questioned were duly impressed with the superiority of the new shaving device, none could explain what was meant by the copywriter's text.[123]

Beginning in the twenties, the application of *art decoratif* (and later on, Bauhaus) styles to product design further intensified the process of mystification. While *art decoratif* had become passé as an expression of high culture, by the mid-thirties many mechanical products had internalized these designs—now called "streamlining."[124] In physics, streamlining was a design that was a "graphical representation of movement. . . . Streamline form is the shape given to a body . . . to the end that its passage through a material may meet with the least resistance."[125] As streamlining became applied to consumption and product design, physics became transformed into cultural allegory—a design which passes through the greatest amount of popular resistance.

Roland Barthes' commentary on the Citroën, then, is not merely a perception of the present, but one rooted deeply in the productive history of industrial capitalism in America. The "benign Nature" (as Barthes calls it) of industrial production is located in such mystifications. It is a benign Nature because it floats or appears to float by virtue of itself. It is a Nature apart from the experience of what is natural.

In the business ideology of the twenties, a benign

Nature was being fashioned and publicized. It was a Nature girded by "Truth" and holding a dream of human happiness molded outside of the realm of human intercourse. Beyond selling goods, American industry was developing and selling a version of current history which extricated the most dangerous element—people—from its process. Change was something which took place on the commodity market, and which was then only mirrored in people's lives. Within such a conception of history and of nature lay the basic element of containment—an implicit denial of its public precept. The contained and orchestrated realities of consumer ideology were testimony to their political imperative. They addressed themselves more to the problem of discontent than they did to how to be content. In each case, the recognition of discontent attempted to channel these impulses into an acceptance of corporate solutions. When Filene spoke of teaching people "how to think" and separated this from any of the "class" traditions of thinking, he was confronting a problem broader than the particular historical *spectre* of bolshevism. He was confronting the problem of people looking amongst themselves for solutions to social ills. The hailing of a "machine civilization" which characterized the ideological formulation of the consumer market cannot be separated from the corporate structure that was attempting to maintain control of the machine by forging a commensurate cultural life.

Consumerism was a world view, a "philosophy of life." But it was not a world view which functioned purely in the economic realm—selling of goods. While it served to stimulate consumption among those who had the wherewithal and desire to consume, it also tried to provide a conception of the good life for those who did not; it aimed at those who were despairing of the possibility of well-being in their immediate industrial environment.

As the ads cleaved all basis for discontent from the industrial context and focused that discontent within realms that offered no challenge to corporate hegemony, they created a vision of social amelioration that depended on adherence to the authority of capitalistic enterprise. Such an adherence was not so much tied up in the actual flow of goods and services, but more in the flow of ideas that commercial propaganda was generating. Only in the instance of an individual ad was consumption a question of *what to buy.* In the broader context of a burgeoning commercial culture, the foremost political imperative was *what to dream.*

THREE

Mom, Dad and the Kids: Toward a Modern Architecture of Daily Life

OUACHITA TECHNICAL COLLEGE

The full force of the attraction of material culture does not show itself with reference to the home until we notice that it is largely responsible for a new type of marriage.

—ERNEST GROVES,
The Drifting Home (1926)

1 Industrialization and the Family: Changing Modes of Survival

The patterns for [the] . . . older way of life remain, but the social-economic situation to which they were addressed has altered. Young men and women face either frustration in their efforts to conform to the older patterns, or confusion and anxiety as they explore for new patterns of conduct. These frustrations are the dominant aspect of the home and family life today.[1]

—LAWRENCE FRANK, member of the
New York City General Education Board (1932).

The politics of consumerism, like those of capitalist society itself, stretched beyond the corral of overt political discord. They also addressed themselves to areas of unrest which were articulated less ideologically. The advancement of consumerism touched on the intimacies of social life, as industry worked to forge a new definition of the family which would mesh with the gears of the productive machine. By the 1920s family life had become contested ground—eroded by increas-

113

ing divorce, its authorities under fire from the women's movement; people felt that what had once sustained an active social life was becoming ineffectual and often painful. The demarcation of what the family should be through advertising represented an attempt at recomposition—redefining family roles so as to bring them in tune with the rhythms of the age. But before going into the ideology of consumption and the family, it is necessary to offer a brief discussion of the context in which such an ideology of recomposition arose.

Preceding industrial development, the relationships, interdependencies and work of family members had been intimately linked to the question of production. Despite its innate oppressiveness and hierarchy, the *patriarchal* family was not a vague ideology spread throughout the society as a "tradition." It was a form of social existence largely determined by the struggle for survival in a predominantly agricultural society faced with chronic scarcity. The authority of the father, his control of much productive initiative and how it was to be implemented, cannot be separated from a situation in which there were few external agencies upon which the family could rely for its existence.[2]

The self-sustaining character of farm life might be seen in the irrelevancy of cash wages as described by a New England farmer's nineteenth-century diary:

> My farm gave me and my whole family a good living on the produce of it and left me, one year with another, one hundred and fifty silver dollars, for I never spent more than ten dollars a year, which was for salt, nails and the like. Nothing to eat, drink or wear was bought, as my farm produced it all.[3]

The family was a unity, patterned around the tasks of production and consumption needs—spheres that were

not discrete. This was the context within which all but
the wealthiest families operated. With the early appearance of factory production, the seeds of transformation
were sown. As industries rose on the American
landscape, they forged not only an "industrial" or
"technological" revolution, but cut deep into the ground
in which the family had been rooted. The first areas of
industry—weaving and textiles—marked a direct transition of home labor into the industrial mode of production. Rather than creating new realms of production
which might add to and coexist with the traditional
realms, early industrialism created a competitive model
in which labors which had been performed in the
isolated domestic sphere or had been limited to small
communities and workshops now found themselves
socially and materially consolidated in the productive
apparatus of the factory.

What occurred in those early days of industry, and
what has marked its history since, has been the steady
displacement of home production by social production,
with the *lore* and *custom* of production formalized and
separated out of the home as planning and engineering. Thus the authority of industry encroached on the
authority of the home whose productive capacity was
becoming outmoded.

By the end of the 1920s, two-thirds of the national
income found its way "across the counters of . . . retail
establishments" selling goods which less than a century
before had been almost totally unrelated to the question
of wages, goods which had been part of the daily
productive capacity of many homes.[4] Where the farmer
of the nineteenth century could account for a ten-dollar
expenditure per annum to supplement what was over-
whelmingly a subsistence living, two-thirds of the national income was now spent on the following: staple

foods, canned and prepared foods, fresh fruit and vegetables (the marketing of these was made possible through improvements in refrigeration techniques), confections, family clothing, furniture, as well as many goods which transcended the *needs* and realms of traditional home production (synthetic cloth, electrical household equipment, radio, and so on).[5] The wage had emerged, in its exchange capacity, as the dominant conduit to survival.

While the definition of the family as interdependent workers in the predominantly agricultural society of the eighteenth and early nineteenth centuries not only defined the idiom of production, but had been the basis of social relationships within the family, the *farming out* of these roles to industry put these social relationships into a state of confusion. The rise of the wage system as a dominant mode of survival meant that a "living" was to be bought and that the social function of work was now mediated by an *exchange process*: selling labor and buying goods. The connection between work and survival still existed, but it was socialized so as to pull the rug of necessity out from under the family as an organization of survival.

Industry was an entrepreneurial venture—conceived and guided by a rising business class. The social relations within the factory were organized according to the priorities of those who controlled it. People entering the factory were involved in a production that was socially organized, but one in which the localized hierarchies of an agrarian culture had been externalized. Social interrelationships had now become part of the structural terminology of factory organization. Each worker was hired as an *individual*; her or his individual labor exchanged for wages. Sustenance turned one's focus from the authority of the family patriarch to the authority of those who generated new forms of survival—the factory owners who provided wages *for a living.* The securing of wages was an isolated contractual arrangement between factory worker and owner, and at least in the minds of the owners, the interdependence and social bonds that continued within working-class culture were subversive of the wage system. While working people struggled to maintain their social basis of work, for the owner the *wage* was a production cost which reduced each worker to a distinct unit in the productive apparatus. The mediation between work and survival made laborers replaceable—by other laborers, or by machines.

By the mid-nineteenth century, capitalism was a productive system in which "wage-slavery" (as the labor movement referred to it) tended to individualize and isolate people in their struggle for survival. Where a pre-industrial (agricultural and artisan) context had necessitated the integral relations of the family and community, the industrial system reified separations.

Men, women and children still worked, but here the work was not an interconnected labor, but a labor sold *individually* for wages in the market. The factory was the basis of social organization and the family of interdependent workers but a relic of the past, devoid of any material underpinnings of necessity beyond their dependency on one another's wage. Stripped of internal necessity the family was weakened, left to the cohesion of emotional bonds. It was now mediated and authorized by the industrial process and the system of wages. The internal authority of the family, as more and more of the workers' world became *bought* rather than *produced*, became symbolic—real for those who experienced it, yet unsupported by the priorities of an industrializing world.

In 1925, writing about the incidence of mothers in industry, sociologist Gwendolyn Hughes found that the wage system significantly defined the nature of social life. "Factory products," she found in her survey of mid-twenties working-class homes in Philadelphia, "supplant home-made commodities, factory labor competes with and displaces household labor, and the family income, instead of being largely *in kind* as formerly, must now take the form of money to pay for the ready-made article." The family, she continued, "is increasingly dependent upon money while the labor resources of its members can be but partially utilized in home production. The less it can produce at home, the more it must spend."[6]

Tendencies toward restriction against child labor did not prevent women and older children from entering industry on an occasional basis: they functioned as they still tend to as a reserve labor force. The inadequacy of fathers' wages combined with industry's demand drew these people from the home. Yet despite this entry of women and older children into the wage system, contemporaneous observers found that the father remained in a special role: invested with the "provider" character of a traditional patriarch, though now adapted to an industrial milieu. This served industry quite well. The notion that *a woman's place is in the home* acted to create an ambivalence among working families as to the propriety of working mothers: it served as an ideological justification for the occasional entry and exit of women into and out of industry. When a larger working population was needed, or the male population was otherwise deployed as during World War I, women entered industry. When the labor market was glutted, the notion of "woman's place" served as a means of trimming the work force without creating "massive unemployment." After all, women were merely reentering their *proper* realm. Yet while that definition of propriety had been born in a patriarchal setting where it had once connoted women's connection to the productive character of the home, in the industrial setting it provided a basis for excluding women from the dominant forms of production. Where a primarily agricultural society had enlisted the work of the entire family, the translation of patriarchy into the industrial context meant that the husband was expected to "assume the greater part of the responsibility for his own support as well as that of another adult and one or two (or more) children."[7] The ideology of the family created a value system which was, in many ways, counter to the economic needs of the family. Throughout the twenties women worked in industry out of the economic necessity that informed their husbands' work, but never with serious acceptance as members of the labor force.

By the 1920s, observers of American society speak unhappily of the widespread sense of rootlessness felt among wide sectors of the population. While the family still provided a widely accepted basis for social life, its erosion as the center of production cut deeply into a whole range of cultural experiences and expectations linked to an earlier life style. Ernest Groves, a leading student of the family in the twenties, wrote of how "a family sense of enterprise was lost and the essential economic task of the family became the problem of distributing an income, usually inadequate, so as to meet the needs and if possible satisfy the desires of its different members." The common interests of the family had shifted from those of "fellow workers in a family environment" to those of discrete "wage-earners."[8]

The spin-offs from such developments were

marked. Divorce between 1870 and the mid-1920s had risen at an unprecedented 35 percent for each ten year period.[9] The causes of the divorce increase were often attributed to the aggravations posed for the home by the industrial world. Chicago School sociologist William Ogburn, along with Groves, felt that "the loss of the economic functions of the home" was conspicuous among these causes.[10] Divorces were indeed more frequent among those most closely wedded to industry and the wage system, as opposed to those whose livelihood remained in subsistence farming or nonindustrial crafts.[11] One first-hand expert, a Judge Bartlett of Reno, Nevada, supported such contentions with the cryptic remark that he saw the "economic factor" as a rising "element in discord."[12] The primacy of the wage within the family cut into a large part of the interdependency that had formerly held it together. While affection remained as a family bond, even this had become implicated within the commodity structure—via advertising which had identified social acceptance with the consumption process. Speaking of the tension facing many relationships in the industrial twenties, Groves and Ogburn concluded that relationships were undergoing a process by which "their vitality is destroyed until eventually they wither."[13]

The money wage, of course, was and is linked to a significant change in the process of production and the definition of work. It elevated a kind of work which was increasingly cleaved from a self-conscious understanding of its relationship to the total process of producing a product. In a situation where a person's job had decreasing significance to the broad question of social survival, and where jobs had become interchangeable parts of a mechanically or bureaucratically defined process, the wage emerged as the clearest connection between the individual worker and the issue of survival.

Writing at the close of the twenties, Lawrence Frank, of the New York City Board of Education, noted that "money income" had become "the focus of endeavor and the only means to a livelihood, in earning which not only men but increasingly women, married and unmarried, are engaged."[14]

The triumph of the wage system, along with its espoused promises of a new and better world, had taken two important social functions out of people's lives. First, it had reduced work to a series of routinized gestures, with knowledge of the whole process increasingly expropriated by industry in the name of organizational rationality—efficiency.[15] Second, the industrialization of production removed the realm of *organization* from the home and community and canonized the centralized, corporate structure as the route through which people's productive lives must travel. Given the separation of workers from these two crucial areas of production, it is not surprising that Frank articulated for these people a feeling that the "helplessness of the individual" had become for the grandchildren of artisans and yeoman farmers the "outstanding characteristic" of the modern condition.[16]

"The creation of products has passed from the home into the factory," noted business researcher Viva Boothe. "The ability of men to provide the necessary products for their families has become indissolubly bound up with the wage system."[17] In terms of the nature of the family's consumption, and the technology of the household, the twenties saw an increasing dependency on factory-wrought wares. Within such a context, the celebration of the home lost much of its footing. The influx of corporate goods and the withering of the productive function of the home had made the tension between the home reality and the home and hearth ideal even more dire.

Within such a historic barrage, the home was a failing refuge. While many people felt the need for those social relations that the home *did* maintain, their own survival required them to look outward for the wage that would maintain the home in a desirable style. Viva Boothe commented on the contradictions in this modern life, specifically as they related to women—the keepers of the homefront in age-old ideology:

> Under present conditions, if the old dictum "The woman's place is in the home" is to be maintained, the husband must become the sole economic contributor to the support of his wife and family in a system where tenure of employment is increasingly insecure, and the wage that he is able to achieve all too frequently, fails to support the family in the style that modern civilization constantly holds out as a possibility. Thus arises the conflict. The old standard dictates a parasitic, non-productive, child-bearing existence for the wife, and further implies that she content herself with lower standards of material comfort and well-being for herself and her family than her environment encourages her to desire.[18]

In order to maintain the home, it became more and more necessary for family members to make sojourns into the world which had been central to its troubles. For men—who maintained the ideological role of *patriarch*—such expeditions were expected and given legitimacy. For women, the entry into the world of business and industry was considered by many to be a violation of morality. Aside from the feminism of the period, the dominant ideology of womanhood in the twenties was one which expected women to "subordinate all other activities to maternity" and other homely roles.[19] Yet the objective reality created a built-in anxiety around such roles. Of the working-class mothers surveyed in the

Hughes study, 20 percent were gainfully employed. When this figure is viewed in terms of the fact that morality and other duties created conditions by which most women "did not remain permanently in industry," the percentage of family women in industry—over a period of time—would be significantly higher.[20] General values and employment practices made women exist as an occasional or reserve work force. When women entered industry, few saw it as a natural calling. In Hughes' survey, only 11 percent of the women interviewed worked out of "personal preference." For the rest (89 percent) the initial appearance of mothers in industry was attributable, in one form or another, to the incapacity of the husband's wages to meet the survival needs of the family.[21] In the mid-twenties the Bureau of Municipal Research of Philadelphia estimated that $25-30 per week was necessary to maintain a "minimum standard of decency for the family of husband, wife, and three children." Three in five working men earned less than $25 per week.[22]

It was from industry rather than the home that the means to family survival were secured and dictated. The axioms of family survival which had fit so neatly into an age of self-sufficiency now seemed inadequate in an age of mass production and an industrialized social network. There was widespread dismay at a world lost, as well as an awareness that what had once made sense no longer meshed with the gears of modern life. It was with these realities in mind that a young person exclaimed:

> What can I do? What should I do? What is worth striving for, amid all this confusion and turmoil?[23]

2 Radical Visions and the Transformation of Patriarchal Authority

While many people lamented the disruptions of modernity, and others looked back to what now appeared to be the more humane conditions of an idealized past, for some the growth of industrial technology and social production heralded a new and libertarian future. Shorn of the harsh realities and stern authorities of a past punctuated by inequity, scarcity and periodic famine, industrialism appeared to have the potential of making possible a future which would meet widespread human needs and abolish the distinct classes of "haves" and "have-nots."

Although dominant trends in American society propagated a Victorian morality which still celebrated and perpetuated the family on the basis of faith, many took issue with such morality. Victorianism had transmitted the Puritan rule of the father and the stern authorities which he symbolized, and carried it into a historical epoch which was making the father less and less of a determining factor on the social landscape.

Where patriarchy had once been supported by the material conditions of society, the rise of capitalism saw it evolve into something like a religion. Such a morality cut the world in two. Where traditional home life had at least theoretically comprised a unity of social existence and production, by the mid-nineteenth century, Victorian moralists such as Catherine Beecher, Sylvester Graham and Sara Josepha Hale (editor of *Godey's Ladies Book*), proclaimed a world of two distinct spheres. On the one side stood the corrupting and masculine world of business; on the other, a *home* ruled by the father and kept moral and virtuous by the mother. Where the home and community had once attempted to comprise a totality of social existence, and patriarchy had been its "legal code," Victorianism elevated the patriarchal home into a spiritual sanctuary against the realities of the productive sphere. Women's work, within the Victorian code, had also moved from the productive to the spiritual. This too signaled the increased externalization of production in an industrial context. Writing in the mid-nineteenth century, Mrs. A. J. Graves projected the increasingly discrete world within which the "American mother shall duly appreciate her domestic responsibilities." The particularly moral and tonic nature of these responsibilities was outstanding.

> . . . our homes shall be made attractive by the pure and satisfying enjoyments which religion, intellect, and the social affections have gathered around them. Then, [she instructed women] . . . when our husbands and our sons go forth into the busy and turbulent world, we may feel secure that they will walk unhurt amid its snares and temptations. Their hearts will be at home, where their treasure is; and they will rejoice to return to its sanctuary of rest, there to refresh their wearied spirits, and renew their strength for the toils and conflicts of life.[24]

While some ventured to canonize the *tradition* of the home, and the moral virtues of womanhood,[25] for others the rise of social production heralded the beginnings of a world which would eclipse the patriarchal yoke itself. In a society in which the material basis of the father's domination was being undercut, the rise of a militant women's movement in the 1840s takes on historic significance. The women's assault on the broad bases of patriarchy coincided with the industrial assault upon that authority. As *equality* was a child of the Enlightenment spirit, so too was it a child of socialized production. Despite Victorian morality, the wage system tended to democratize the relationship between individuals (both men and women, if commonly employed in industry) and the society. The example of early feminism points to the dialectical quality of the turn toward social production. While this turn disrupted relationships severely and exacted arduous labor for little compensation, it also began to create a productive machinery and social vision which pointed to an end to the conditions which had given material sustenance to social domination.

By the twentieth century, some who wrote of industrialism saw a reconstitution of social relations which would transcend both pre-industrial patriarchy and the Victorian morals which had tried to replace it. For some, the development of industrial production pointed not only to the supersession of paternal authority, but to oppressive social control *per se*. Thorstein Veblen, throughout his life, held the conviction that while entrepreneurial activities and domination had been essential to the assembling of a technological apparatus, the role of finance had become outmoded and now *held back* the liberating potential of a technological society.[26]

Focusing more on the internal structures of social life, some feminists spoke to the possibility of liberating relations between the sexes from the traditions which had long governed the history of scarcity. Charlotte Perkins Gilman, writing around 1900, spoke optimistically of an end to the "sexuo-economic" conditions which had traditionally forced women to exchange sexual favors for livelihood and had separated them from the productive potentiality of industrial society. In a direct critique of Victorian patriarchy, Gilman argued that women's creative capacities had been stifled,

> confined to the level of immediate bodily service, to the making of clothes and preparing of food for individuals. No social service is possible. While its power of production is checked, its power of consumption is inordinately increased by the showering upon it of the "unearned increment" of masculine gifts. For the woman there is, first, no free production allowed; and, second, no relation maintained between what she does produce and what she consumes.[27]

The domination of the patriarch within the traditional arenas of production had created in women, Gilman argued, an "over-developed sex-nature." By this, she was referring to female sexuality as a forced medium of exchange which patriarchal "wisdoms" had made women cultivate. As industrial, or *social*, production supplanted the traditional patriarchy, Gilman saw the creation of new, democratic possibilities:

> While the sexuo-economic relation makes the family the centre of industrial activity, no higher collectivity than we have to-day is possible. But, as women become free economic, social factors, so becomes possible the full social combination of individuals in collective industry. With such freedom, such independence, such wider union, becomes possible also a union between man and woman such as the world has long dreamed of in vain.[28]

Novelist Floyd Dell, in his study of *Love in the Machine Age*, carried this feminist-humanist-industrial argument into the context of mass production. Writing in 1930, Dell said that the possibility of production to meet historically unmet needs had brought about the opportunity to coalesce the romantic ideal of love with the reality of a world which could sustain it—devoid of sexual *exchange*. "Modern machinery," he contended, "has laid the basis for a more biologically normal family life than has existed throughout the whole of the historical period, or indeed in the whole life of mankind."[29] Giving support to Gilman's "long dreamed of . . . union between man and woman," Dell argued that "modernity reestablishes family life on the basis of romantic love."[30]

While Dell was aware that new authorities might rise, he and others tended to sense a positive change in the social order. To them, wage labor and industrial production extricated people from the arenas of production which had bred patriarchal domination. Likewise, the liberating abundance which they saw the industrial machinery capable of producing would ultimately challenge the irrationalities and inequities of the wage system itself.

Businessmen had a different view of the future. While most radicals hailed the decline of traditional family structure as a guidepost to a nonauthoritarian future, American industrial thought tended to look toward a recomposed conception of authority. The decline of pre-industrial patriarchy had been integral to industrial ascendency, yet the adaptation of Victorian family ideology to the commodity context seemed integral to the maintenance of a reconstituted patriarchy.

3 The Family as Ground for Business Enterprise

While sociologists lamented the loosening bonds of family life, businessmen in the twenties saw the phenomenon as an essential part of their own rise to dominance. Utilizing the lingo of feminism, insofar as it connoted an equal status for men and women vis-à-vis corporate domination, Edward Filene wrote:

> . . . since the head of the family is no longer in control of the economic process through which the family must get its living, he must be relieved of many ancient responsibilities and therefore of many of his prerogatives. . . . Women . . . and children are likely to discover that their economic well-being comes not from the organization of the family but from the organization of industry, and they may look more and more for individual guidance, not to their fathers, but to the *truths* which science is discovering.[31]

The welcome demise of familial authority was at the core of his pronouncement, yet his argument was not directed at the existence of authority itself. Rather it pointed toward the commodity market and its propaganda to replace the father's authority. Business was to provide the source of a life style, where before the father had been the dictator of family spirit.

No less an authority than Calvin Coolidge heralded the spiritual ascendency of the business patriarch: "the man who builds a factory builds a temple . . . and it is there, in the shadow of the industrial altar, that worship must shift."[32]

Underscoring the historical inevitability of corporate domination over the breadth of modern life, Filene put business within a continuum which included the roles of the family and the republic. "Just as the institution of the family developed most of the human qualities which we have come to hold most precious, and just as the institution of the state developed patriotism and a wider human consciousness," he reasoned, the "new order of business is developing a more inclusive loyalty, a sense of oneness of all humanity, and is already making human selfishness function unselfishly for the common good on a world scale."[33]

In many ways Filene accepted the widespread sense of family dislocation, yet gave it a new grounding and a firm and positive spiritual role within the shadow of the corporate patriarchy which was to replace it. The depreciation of the father, whose power had been located in the "intrinsic necessity of the direct form of dependence for the life process of [the old] society,"[34] was couched in terms of a new and benevolent order. It was an order which would free women and children from the stern dictates of the traditional patriarch, yet would replace these with the dictates of industry, which like the father of the Victorian morality, demanded an "inclusive loyalty."

The industrial inroads into family structure coincided with the rise of mass industrial production and employment. As the goods of industry increasingly called for mass distribution, and as the scope of industry encompassed a growing proportion of the population, the world of business became more concerned with the question of how social life and family life coincided with the demands of industrial production, consumption and the broad issue of social order. Henry Ford, who had pioneered in the mass production of goods, also pioneered in the extension of industrial authority to family relations. Ford, through his "Sociology Department," entered the homes of his workers to ensure their fidelity to his concept of proper living. While many of the values enforced by this department seem counter to the values of spendthrift consumerism (thrift, sobriety and religion were Ford's central values), the important thing about this practice was not its particularly puritanical bent. For central to Ford's philosophy was the assumption that the corporation had assumed a right to administer, directly, family matters. Antonio Gramsci, an Italian social critic writing in the late twenties, had this to say about the patriarchal-corporatism inherent in "Fordism" (while focusing on Ford's sexual ideology, Gramsci's statement may be applied to the whole of the question of social life):

> It is worth drawing attention to the way in which industrialists (Ford in particular) have been concerned with the sexual affairs of their employees and with their family arrangements in general. One should not be misled, any more than in the case of prohibition, by the "puritanical" appearance assumed by this concern. The truth is that the new type of man demanded by the rationalization of production and work cannot be developed until the sexual instinct has been suitably regulated and until it too has been rationalized.[35]

As the industrialization of American society and the decomposition of traditional family bonds gave rise to radical libertarian thought, it became all the more important for industrial ideology itself to be agile. Given the antisocial character of a productive system which had routinized work into a series of time-managed, mechanical gestures, the family—the scene of leisure and consumption—continued to be a repository of social relations. For the radicals as well as the newly conscious ideologues of business, the image of the family characterized the good life. Yet while Gilman and Dell had seen the family as a reinvigorated soil for romantic affection, no longer economically defined, the attitudes of business saw it as soil for more profitable growth. Countering an ideology which envisioned the reconciliation of love and affection, people in the business community maintained an economic view of the subject. For them, *love* appeared a realm for entrepreneurial excavation. Romanticism, which from its medieval inception had posed as a critical alternative to patriarchal authority, now appeared in two distinct forms. While some radicals saw it as the kernel of a nonauthoritarian future, businessmen saw it as a profitable weapon against an outmoded authority in favor of a new one.

Christine Frederick, who had inveighed against the formation of consumer protective organizations, saw "a direct and vital business interest in the subject of young love and marriage." Trying to reconcile the continuation of the family with the home inculcation of industrial values, she spoke to her businessman colleagues in straightforward terms:

> Every business day approximately 5,000 new homes are begun; new "nests" are constructed and new

> family purchasing units begin operation. . . . The
> founding and furnishing of new homes is a major
> industrial circumstance in the United States.[36]

Houses themselves reflected this circumstance. Observers of home architecture in the twenties noted that the traditional spaces which had been used for home production were vanishing in new houses. As canning, bread-baking, sewing, cleaning and dyeing left the home, houses were built to accommodate the steady flow of goods through its cupboards. "The family dwelling," noted William F. Ogburn in a report to a presidential commission, "tells something as to the economic functions carried on within." Speaking of the modern home as compared to those of the past, Ogburn noted a clear shrinking of space for families as their productive capacities decreased. Between the end of World War I and the end of the twenties, the size of apartments in Chicago shrank by 25 percent. Construction of apartments above five rooms shrank from 25 percent to 8 percent over the same period of time. Kitchens gave way to kitchenettes in four out of ten apartments in a survey of twenty-six major cities.[37] The redesignation of the home as an arena primarily of consumption concretely relates to Frederick's sanguinity on the promulgation of "young love."

Clearly, Frederick's exhortation to business to take an interest in the continuation of the family was based on an understanding that the industrial recomposition of the family must be accomplished in modernistic terms. The extension of credit to the family, she argued, would not only increase the ability to consume, but would also subsidize the home role of women who should, she felt, *direct* much of this consumption. Speaking for business, she felt that "consumer credit" was a way to "break new ground" in socializing the family to the idiom of mass-produced life. It was a way of "capitalizing the new home" both ideologically and economically; it would assure the imposition of consuming tendencies couched in agreeable terms "made with the young couple themselves."[38] While the cultivation of the home was always spoken of with reverence for the *family*, it was in fact characterized by the shift of authority away from the family. Love, like democracy, had become implicated in a broad patriotic program which revolved around the mass distribution of commodities, focusing the human psyche on the issue of accumulating goods as a primary social bond and activity.

It is interesting that much of the business definition of the reconstituted family structure borrows from the critique of the decomposed family—at times underscoring the decline of the father's authority and mouthing conceptions of women's emancipation. Yet while radical ideas spoke for a new collectivity, the way in which such questions were enmeshed in the wage system made the business version of reconstituted family life singularly noncollective. Taking issue with the notion of the family as a *consuming unit*, Robert Lynd concluded that "consuming unit was a misnomer in that it implied a modicum of collectivity." Instead, Lynd argued, the involvement of the family bond within the wage-consumption process had equated it with the basic premise of "free labor." As each wage earner confronted work as an individual selling his labor, the consumerized family had undergone a "devolution" through buying, into an "increasingly loosely articulated group that we call the family."[39] Traditionally the family had found a social bond, a collectivity in its production and self-definition of activity. But within the mass industrial context, it was the "productive and merchandising agencies" which increasingly acted in concert, while "the consumer faces his problems alone."[40] The conditions of the family member, despite the continuation of a family ethos, exacted a personal, individualized relationship to the burgeoning authority of business enterprise. Though separated from one another, the conditions of production and the conditions of consumption were simultaneously mirrored in a newly espoused ideology where the *proper* roles of the family members required *individual* faith in the authority of business.

The extraction of children from the work force had multiplied the need for such faith. Where children as workers took their place in the production and survival functions of the family, the creation of childhood and adolescence—a period of time with none but a consumptive relationship to civil society—demanded that parents rely on external socializing agencies, as much of their own time was spent at work. Once a financial credit, modern childhood was a debit on the family— increasingly involving it in the consumption of goods and services connected to child-rearing. To many in the twenties, the association of children with the increase in external influence was clear. Working-class families of *Middletown* spoke of how children carried into the home the messages of growing industrial authority and the industrialized moralities of home economics, movies, Y's, and education in general. As children brought home such messages, and argued for their expanded realm of consumption within the distribution of family wages, parents felt these forces "drawing the child away from the home." It is not surprising that many working families in *Middletown* expressed the feeling that consumption of goods and services by children had provided a conduit between the family as an arena of social relations and external agencies seen to be "an 'enemy' of the home and society."[41]

An ad for *True Story* magazine (1924), a Macfadden
publication directed at a solidly working-class audience,
based its appeal on the transfer of authority from the
home to the wisdom of mass enterprise:

> Until five years ago there was nowhere men and
> women, boys and girls could turn to get a knowledge
> of the rules of life. They were sent out into the world
> totally unprepared to cope with life. . . . Then came
> *True Story*, a magazine that is different from any ever
> published. Its foundation is the solid rock of truth.
> . . . It will help you, too.[42]

Capitalizing on the sense of *helplessness* that had
marked the confusion of the modern family, and dis-
missing the old homemaking techniques and "finger
knowledge" as anachronistic where they persisted, the
ad directed its readers to accept the family as a context
rather than a source for socialization. It was through the
vehicles of mass industrial production that cement for
modern relations would be provided; it was through
these relations that allegiance to capitalism would be
elicited.

The nominal continuation of the traditional roles—
like *mom*, *dad* and *the kids*—was assured, but the definition of these now tended to substantiate the rise of
corporate authority. A look at the presentation of these
roles, the characterization of "youth," the father, the
mother, and their functional definition by businessmen
and their advertising will give more substance to the
changes in *architecture** that the family underwent.

* I have chosen the term *architecture* carefully, although it may be
misleading. I am not speaking, except where so indicated, of housing *per se*.
Rather, by *architecture*, I mean the unity of structure and fashion. This is
characteristic both of housing and of social relations in the modern family as
they were related to the evolving commodity market.

4 Youth as an Industrial Ideal

To businessmen, the reconstituted family would be one which maintained its reproductive function, but which had abandoned the dogma of parental authority, except insofar as that *authority* could be controlled and provide a conduit to the process of goods consumption. While attempts were being made to legislate child labor out of the marketplace in the opening decades of the twentieth century,[43] the symbolic role of youth was central to business thought. The fact that childhood was increasingly a period of consuming goods and services made *youth* a powerful tool in the ideological framework of business. Beyond the transformation of the period of childhood and adolescence into a period of consumption, youth was also a broad cultural symbol of renewal, of honesty, and of criticism against injustice—the young have always provided a recurrent rejection of the ancient *virtues* of "the establishment" at times when more mature citizens consent and sit back.

The concept of youth was, at the same time, an

instrumentation of modern control. The significance of youth within an industrial society was central both to the change in production and the shift in authority. These two questions were inextricably linked to the status of *skill* in the modern industrial process.

Speaking of the traditional avenues of authority, one industrial worker noted in 1924 that "when tradition is a matter of the spoken word, the advantage is all on the side of age. The elder is in the saddle." Helen and Robert Lynd added that age demands respect "when tradition is a matter of elaborate learned skills of hand and eye." They noted, however, that "machine production is shifting traditional skills from the spoken word and the fingers of the master craftsmen of the Middletown of the nineties to the cams and levers of the increasingly versatile machine."[44] During the rapid rationalization of production that was seen in the period following 1910, material conditions emerged which threatened the basis of community and family hierarchy and challenged it with a hierarchy which followed the mechanical and pecuniary imperatives of business enterprise. Particularly in the period between the two World Wars, technological historian Siegfried Giedion has noted, "this much is certain: at one sweep, mechanization penetrates the intimate spheres of life. What the preceding century and a half had initiated, and especially what had been germinating from mid-nineteenth century on, suddenly ripens and meets life with its full impact."[45]

The penetration into the "intimate spheres of life" was an incision into age-old realities of production and the kinds of work and oral traditions of skill which they had encompassed. By the mid-1920s, the loss of such traditions was widely felt. Where artisan and agricultural labors had required a period of long training, leading toward a life-time resource to draw upon, the rapidity of the machine had made the worker an adjunct to its rhythms. The "swiftness and endurance" required of a machine-tender had displaced the "training and skill" of "the apprentice-master-craftsman system" within the few years that had seen the wide-scale implementation of industrial line work.[46] Most young people spoke of how they would "stumble on" or "fall into" jobs that were to "become literally their life's work." Their strength, and not their skill, was what was appealing to employers.[47]

The rise of *youth*, or the endurance of youth, as a central qualification for employment was sorely felt in the laments of working people in *Middletown*:

> Whenever you get old [said one forty-year-old laborer], they are done with you. The only thing a man can do is to keep as young as he can and save as much as he can.

> One woman spoke frankly about how youth was her family's most precious commodity. Speaking of her husband, she prophesied, "He is forty and in about ten years now will be on the shelf. . . ." She added that "We are not saving a penny but we are saving our boys."[48]

The crisis of age was severe enough, and youthful endurance short enough, to punctuate an entire lifetime of anxiety over the question of youth. Three *Middletown* wives spoke of the premature aging that the system had laid upon their husbands, ages 26, 40, and 30 respectively:

> There's nothing ahead where he's at and there's nothing to do about it.
> There won't never be anything for him as long as he stays where he is and I don't know where else he can go.

He'll never get any better job. He'll be lucky if they keep him on this one.[49]

In each case, the endurance required by monotonous factory work had laid a severe economic and psychological burden on the lives of working people. Youth had provided an idiom for the transformation in production, and the elevation of the *youth* value within the culture had provided an ideological weapon against the traditional realms of indigenous authority as it had been exercised in the family and community in the periods before mass production. Youth ultimately became a language of control; instead of being used in the critical and rebellious sense that we associate with it today, it was, in the words of Floyd Dell, but a modernized interpretation of "the old patriarchal wish to exploit the younger generation's . . . life for economic purposes."[50]

Despite the decline in child labor as a result of protective legislation and the decline of the apprenticeship system, mechanized production depended heavily on the endurance and reflexes of youth. While in the 1930s the period of employment began later in life than it had thirty years before, it was in young adulthood that industry sought its ideal of the "efficient worker." Age, once a sign of accumulated productive know-how, had become a detriment; compulsory retirement signified the transformation of labor from craftsmanship to unskilled, machine-tending.[51] As the culture devalued age as an ideal, much of the population was affected. While the first quarter of the century had seen a greater percentage of people living beyond the age of sixty-five, the percentage in that age group that found itself gainfully employed decreased.[52] Thus the allegedly progressive implementation of American technology had a serious flaw: its operation required a definition of worker which pushed older folks out of the factory and away from the means to a livelihood, while these older people represented an increasingly large proportion of the American people.

Advertising was a prime source of the idealization of youth. As youth appeared the means to industrial survival, its promulgation as something to be *achieved* by consumption provided a bridge between people's need for satisfaction and the increased corporate priorities of mass distribution and worker endurance. Beyond this, the celebration of youth was also an idealization of innocence and malleability.

Max Horkheimer spoke of the way in which the development of a centralized, corporate authority made use of the concept of youth. The idealization of youth asked fathers and mothers to abandon their favored positions and to turn their adoration toward the qualities of their children. Giving direct analysis of the transformation in patriarchy that corporate authority entailed, Horkheimer explained:

> Now the rapidly changing society which passes its judgment upon the old is represented not by the father, but by the child. The child, not the father, stands for reality.[53]

The important productive role of youth, combined with the pleasure-seeking conception of youth, called for the child as a representative of a desirable reality. Yet this cultural canonization of youth had little to do with any actual power moving from parent to child. Rather, it represented the new industrial priorities within the traditional mode of survival: the family.

Advertising directed some of its messages directly at children, preferring their "blank slate" characters to those of their parents whose prejudices might be more developed. J. B. Watson, the psychologist/ad man, had given underpinning to such a strategy. If the children were indoctrinated in the "behavioristic freedom" which characterized the modern industrial world, he argued, business might be able to intervene in the values and definitions of family culture. Rejecting the "freedom of the libertine"—as he called attitudes which were not responsible to industrial reality—he spoke for an education of children into the categories of modern life. If this could be done, he felt that children could help to circumvent parental attitudes which were not in step with the exigencies of the industrial process. "Will not these children in turn," he asked rhetorically, "with their better ways of living and thinking, replace us as society, and in turn bring up" yet more modern children?[54]

Alfred Poffenberger, a leading advertising psychologist, spoke for directing advertising at children. Confronted with "the great difficulty that one meets in breaking habits" among their parents, he underscored the "importance of introducing innovations by way of the young."[55]

Where ads were not written directly for the young, they often spoke in the name of the young against parental attitudes. Chiding nonconsuming parents for less than adequate care of their offspring, ads spoke of their products as essential for survival of children in the modern world. A 1929 ad for Quaker Oats pictured young "James Folan," who "led his class last year and checked 100% in health tests too." In a letter, written presumably by his mother, comes a formula for such success: "Our mornings are never too rushed to give Jimmy his Quick Quaker Oats breakfast."[56] The question of performance and health in a child were never far from the institutions that judged her/him from outside of the family circle: today it was school, in ten years, her or his employer. The concept of the successful youth provided a definition of the successful adult—one who performs well in the eyes of an institution.

Following the logic of the *Middletown* woman who spoke of having no savings but was "saving our boys," this industrial youth ethic was underscored by an ad for the Yale lock company. The ad depicted a mother holding a baby and was captioned, "Yale guards your treasures."[57] While many older people were suffering a feeling of increasing irrelevance, ads and the industries they represented spoke up for the child. The child was a representation of endurance at work and the unification of consumption and the pleasure principle. Intimating a greater concern for the child than mere parents could possibly have, the Pepsodent company admonished parents of 1922 with the question, "Shall They Suffer as you did from film on teeth?" Implying that film on the teeth was known about, much less suffered by parents, the ad conveyed the message that the needs of the child were better understood by industry. Such ads were a microcosm of the attempt to shift authority in a mass industrial world.

The ads of the twenties, however, were not predominantly concerned with actual children. Youth flourished, rather, as a symbolic representation of cultural change; of a change which meant that now "a boy of nineteen may, after a few weeks of experience on a machine, turn out an amount of work greater than his father of forty-five."[58] It represented a change which prompted Abraham Myerson, a physician specializing in the problems of neurotic women, to make the following comments regarding the widespread feeling of displacement and uselessness among adult women:

> Throughout the community there is a stir and excitement that is reflecting on the children. There are so many desirable luxuries in the world now, so many revealed by [the mass culture]. . . .
> All these things make the lot of the housewife harder in so far as the training of her children is concerned. She is dealing with a more alert, more sophisticated, more sensuous child—and one who knows his place and power. . . . And a wise old gentleman said to his grandson recently, when the lad complained about his mother, "Of course you are right. Every son has a right to be obeyed by his mother."[59]

While this displacement of parents has caused one recent historian, Gilman Ostrander, to proclaim the 1920s a true period of "filiarchy"—rule by the young—[60]the truth is more complex. The symbolic ascendency of youth represents the corporate infiltration of daily life and the creation of a family structure that might be ruled through the young, or through people's acceptance of a youthful ideal. In pursuing youth, people would forsake indigenous patriarchal authorities and accept malleability, endurance and individualism as positive values. The laments of those who were feeling old at forty were met by advertisements such as one for Sun•Maid Raisins, which indicated that an acceptance of modern consumption could keep people "*young* . . . at fifty."[61]

Youth was an industrial ideal, a growing category of modern work and survival, and its approximation was being sold through the retail markets of nationally advertised brands. Corporations which demanded youth on the production line now offered that same youth through their products. Whatever goods were for sale, the promise that adults could perform like children was essential to the messages of many ads. Speaking to the sales force of a large cosmetics firm, Helen Woodward said, "Remember that what we are selling is not beauty—it is youth." Moreover, she was explicit about what kind of youth—one which was mass-produced and could *only* be bought. "We are going to sell every artificial thing there is. . . . And above all things it is going to be young—young—young! We make women feel young."[62]

Adults were instructed to look toward youth for an "in-step" understanding of what was right and proper to the new age. Yet the look toward youth was but a mediation for the corporate priorities which youth came to symbolize. Children's subconscious minds were depicted as infiltrated by the commodity market, and parents in the ads were supposed to accept and be sensitive to that invasion. A 1922 ad for Jell-O showed a little girl sitting in her mother's lap, her face filled with terror. Having just awoken from a bad dream she bares her commodified soul:

> The nightmare mother! I was dreaming that Jimmie stole my Jell-O.[63]

Elsewhere, the ads often painted a picture of adults as incompetent in coping with modernity, and raised the model of youth as a conduit for consumption. A 1922 ad from Paramount studios documented the breakdown of parental know-how and gives an insight into the ways in which youth served as a cover for new authorities. Reinforcing the need for "keeping up with youngsters," the ad resolved that "the young folks do their parents every bit as much good as their parents do them." Yet the benefit of youthful leadership was not far from the directives of the marketplace. In explaining the progressive role of the younger generation, the ad expounded that "were it not for the children, some of you parents would not know even now what a tremendous change for the better Paramount has [made] in motion pictures."[64]

When one looks at the composition of the major audiences of motion pictures in the twenties, the industrial ethic of such an ad becomes more apparent. In a study of consumption patterns of 1931, the Heller Committee, under the direction of Dr. Jessica B. Peixotto (University of California), found that while professional families—favoring live theatre and music—spent an average of $11.28/year on the movies, working-class and low-wage clerical (white collar) families spent $22.56/year at the cinema. These figures show that despite incomes of between one-fourth and one-third below those of professional families, wage-earning families tended to spend twice as much on movies.[65] All of this underscores the largely working-class audience toward which the ad was directed, and for which the ideal of *its own* corporatized *youth* was being presented.

Given the challenge to survival that the *youth* question posed for working people in the twenties, the continual promise of youth is more than an offer of a clear complexion. Rather, it is an offer of that which was increasingly demanded by the industrial process, and that which was sorely felt among the older (twenty-five-plus) working population of *Middletown*. All surfaces and orifices were potential gardens in which *youth* might be rekindled. Nujol, a feminine douche, indicated that through a program of internal cleanliness, one might achieve the superficial appearance of that which was increasingly in demand: "A clear, radiant, youthful complexion."[66] Resinol Soap told its users that they might expect to *look* "like a new person!"[67] Hinds Cream users could have "skin . . . like a baby's" and Palmolive Soap could mimic a "school-girl complexion."[68]

This emulation of the child was one that implied unabashed involvement in and commitment to prescribed patterns of consumption. The ideal was one of irrepressible, frantic energy. The *flapper*, whom Christine Frederick described in 1929 as having evolved into the modern mother, was an expression of such an ideal and was ubiquitous in advertising of the twenties.[69] She was pure consumer, busy dancing through the world of modern goods. She was *youth*, marked by energy not judgment. Her clothes, her vehicles, her entire milieu were mass-produced—and she liked it.

The evolution of American industry had moved to a point where the canonization of youth provided a two-pronged support for its institutions. First it undercut a patriarchal family, insofar as that family had located industrial knowledge within its own community. As work became increasingly appended to the machine, the elevation of certain characteristics of youth gave affirmation to a concrete and often devastating change in the process of production. Likewise, the elevation of youth, and the reality of youthful endurance, made *youngness* a desirable and salable commodity. People's anxieties over the turn in production were now focused toward a safe solution. Youth could be bought, or so the ads claimed. Once again, the loci of social unrest were being confronted in the marketplace.

5 Father: The Patriarch as Wage Slave

A woman's place was widely defined as in the home, just as the father was defined by his duties and activities *outside* of the family unit. His role was seen as that of provider and producer within the new industrial order. The home, the arena of consumption, was central to the woman's world and consequently only a small percentage of advertising appears to have been directed at the male population.[70] However, certain products did address themselves primarily to men. When they did, they too underscored the decline of a materially based patriarchal authority, presenting the rise of corporate control of daily life as a given.

Within a context where, as Filene had observed, "the head of the family is no longer in control of the economic process through which the family must get its living,"[71] the maxims of patriarchal authority had little grounding. A pre-industrial patriarchy had engendered the following kind of familial hierarchy, as ratified in

The Token of Friendship, or Home, The Center of Affections
(1844):

> The father gives his kind command,
> The mother joins, approves;
> The children all attentive stand,
> Then each obedient moves.[72]

By the 1920s, however, such paternal authority had become more and more ceremonial and many saw the tradition of male direction and aggressiveness as fallen ideals. Lawrence Frank, raising questions about the problems of male adulthood, cut through to the intimate crisis within the patriarchal expectation. "The young man who would fulfill the older conception of a competent male, ambitious, enterprising, prepared to support a wife and family, faces a most perplexing situation," he reported. For the male, "the discrepancy between the patterns offered him by a [patriarchal] tradition . . . and the changing social-economic conditions gives rise to acute anxiety and perplexity."[73] Pointing ultimately to the question of male potency, Frank described the unhappy plight of a fallen ideal and the contradictions that it faced.

The sense of a crisis over the viability of patriarchy was widespread in the social literature of the twenties, and people in business were well aware of such a development; characteristically they spoke to its pecuniary possibilities. Discussing the new inroads which might be made via a direct appeal to woman consumers, Christine Frederick related these inroads to the decrepit state of masculinity. Associating masculinity with aggressive self-direction and femininity with passive receptivity—surely classical sexual characterizations—Frederick announced the changes as they related to a culture of mass consumption. "The Anglo-Saxon male tradition is slipping!" she declared. Referring to the ways in which mass industrialism increasingly relied on women as a focus for its social values, she exclaimed that "our civilization is lush soil for the feminine, but barren soil for the masculine characteristics." Elucidating this judgment, she explained that while men seem to be good workers in the modern society, "in general the American man . . . is not especially competent at personal or family purchasing," i.e., men were less and less able to bear responsibility for defining the material character of the social environment in which they lived.[74] Thus while women were cultivated as general purchasing managers for the household, the basic definition of *men* in the ads was as bread-winners, wage-earners. *Man's* role was divested of all social authority, except insofar as his wages underwrote family consumption. At the same time women were elevated to a managerial status, forming the link between wages and the historical character of survival. The entrapment in the wage system was undisputed and even reinforced by the ads.

Even where the father was held as a fallen symbol of authority, it was an authority which was founded on his money-earning capacity, not his social power. In a series of ads for the Prudential Life Insurance Company, the definition of father was reduced to a purely earning function. As such, the money that an insurance company might provide a fatherless family was couched in terms which depicted the company as an ample father substitute. One such ad, appearing in 1925, showed a widowed mother visiting her children in an "Orphan Asylum." Characteristic of a concept of *youth* where it is the children who define reality, it is the child who reveals the "truth" about *father*. The asylum authorities, says the child in the ad, had "said father didn't keep his life insurance paid up." It is the child who carries the banner of the company, implying that good fathers take out good insurance policies to take their place when they are "gone." At the bottom of the ad appears the Rock of Gibraltar—the Prudential trademark—standing firm as a new patriarchal symbol; one which locates stability and social survival in corporate hands.[75]

Another Prudential ad[76] showed a mother and child, their faces wrought with despair, between them a photograph of the deceased father. Facing the problem of a foreclosed mortgage, the ad once again underscored the father as wage-earner, the family as a nonproductive assembly of consumers, and Prudential as an ample father substitute, a way in which the family might continue its consuming functions (survival).

The message of many ads of the twenties placed living fathers centrally within the often capricious wiles of modern employment. As work became less a matter of accumulated skill and more a question of loyal diligence to the task, consumption was depicted as the way men would be able to objectify that diligence within themselves. It was around the question of how a man might establish his image that the tenure of employment might be ensured. Where work, particularly industrial work, required little beyond endurance and fidelity, it was on the symbolic level that success and failure were pitted against one another. An ad for Edgeworth Pipe Tobacco (1929) showed a worker pointing to his boss. Answering a question, he indicates, "The Boss? . . . There, with th' pipe." The connection between *boss* and *pipe* offered a promise of security to those who were still nonpipe smokers. "Men at the top are apt to be pipe-smokers. Ever noticed," chided the ad. "It's no mere coincidence—pipe-smoking is a calm and deliberate habit—restful, stimulating. His pipe helps a man think straight. A pipe is back of most big ideas."[77]

With industry increasingly invading the interstices of social life and with work having become characterized more by a person's ability to keep to a routine than by his or her prowess, there was little about *a job* which could make a person feel indispensable and little in the way of self-definition that could make a person feel that what he was doing could not be done just as well by someone else. Thus, particularly in ads directed at men, things like personal appearance or an image of dedication were the things which might distinguish one person from another. Productive competition for jobs was integrated within the ideology of a consumer market which was offering men a means to success. By smoking a pipe, or by looking a certain way, people could accumulate the social appearance necessary in a world which had placed a decreasing value on creative skills.

The ads also indicated that where job-dissatisfaction occurred, it was often a result of personal inadequacies combined with insufficient consumption. Blue-Jay Corn Plasters told men about a fellow whose painful corn "cost him his job," even though he was generally "the best-natured man on the pay-roll. Nothing seemed to faze his good humor." Here, this man's body turns against him: a corn. And "then came the amazing blow-up," which got him fired. Here the Listerine dictum that people should "suspect themselves first" entered the question of job conditions and satisfaction. To keep a job, people must love it; they must fight against those things *in themselves* which get in the way of job satisfaction. They must consume to keep healthy and stay healthy to keep their jobs. Obedience was tied to health, "blow-ups" would come from corns.

The wage process had dictated labor to be sold,

regardless of its recognizable connection to the productive process. As labor was sold, an alleged substitute for job satisfaction came to be bought, since it could not be felt, and men vied with one another through their skill at assembling bought surfaces and images in a labor market defined by exchange. Men were encouraged to buy according to the categories of job security, much as women were encouraged to buy in order to ensure home security for themselves.

Where appearances gave way to the actual demands of industrial work, the categories of achievement and effective performance were offered for sale. Postum could turn grouchy husbands into mild mannered "achievers"; in an age of emotional duress, a particular cereal beverage could keep men from "cracking up physically, in the race for success."[78] The California Fruit Growers' Exchange offered a cure for "acidosis" —a mystified term for low vitality—to men whose last skill *was* their vitality. Of the man who does not eat oranges and lemons, it was asked rhetorically, "I don't know why that fellow doesn't get ahead."[79]

For the male, the ideals of domination and self-direction were wilted under the blinding authority of corporate survival. No longer able to rely on the skills of production, men were channeled into an idiom defined by a much more passive skill. At Christmas time 1929, the Hamilton Watch Company told wives to buy their husbands a watch for a present. As time had been mechanized by the factory process, a good watch became a key to success.

> He tells you that he really doesn't *want* anything for Christmas. But there's one thing he may need and not realize it.
> Many times a day as he struggles for success in

business* he may be hampered by a watch he himself only half trusts.

Yet every investigation proves that the successful man is time-minded—accuracy minded. Time to him means money. Every minute must work. His watch must be accurate.

That's where your help comes in! Give him a watch upon which he can rely *completely* . . . a watch that will help him get ahead, and so bring you both happiness."[80]

Christmas was an occasion when the sentiment of gift-giving, the priority of consumption, and the category of industrial punctuality might be merged. The fête had been invested with a new *universality*, defined in the totality of mass industrial categories. Advertising constantly reminded men, and women who bought things for men, that their needs had been implicated in a new realm of experience and that the process of self-definition should constantly link the realm of consumption to the wage-earning capacity called "survival."

* Here, as elsewhere, "business" is a euphemism for work.

6 Consumption and the Ideal of the *New* *Woman*

The twenties saw little movement away from the basic attitude that the domain of women was the home. Despite wide-spread employment of women in industry from World War I on, the general expectation was that "women [should] . . . subordinate all activities to maternity," and, as Gwendolyn Hughes lamented in 1925, it was still "generally assumed that wage-earning by mothers is detrimental to the race."[81] Contrary to this, the prevalent feminist position followed Olive Schreiner's conception of women which proclaimed an equalization of the sexes as a promise and imperative of industrial life. "We demand," she announced, "that in the strange new world that is arising upon the man and woman, where nothing is as it was, and all things are assuming new shapes and relations, that in this new world we also shall have our share of honored and socially useful human toil."[82] Yet the passage of the suffrage amendment had taken much wind out of the more libertarian and militant strains of feminism, and the prevalent association of women and the home persevered. Looking at the ads of the 1920s, one sees how the feminist demand for equality and freedom for women was appropriated into the jargon of consumerism. A classic example of commercialized feminism was a 1929 campaign in which the American Tobacco Company attempted "to induce women to smoke [cigarettes] in public places." George W. Hill, owner of American Tobacco had contracted Edward Bernays to run the campaign, hoping to expunge the "hussy" label from women who smoked publicly. The smoking taboo among women, Bernays reasoned, was of deep psychological significance. Accordingly, he consulted the psychoanalyst, A.A. Brill, for advice. Brill's explanation was this:

> "Some women regard cigarettes as symbols of freedom. . . . Smoking is a sublimation of oral eroticism; holding a cigarette in the mouth excites the oral zone. It is perfectly normal for women to want to smoke cigarettes. Further the first women who smoked probably had an excess of masculine components and adopted the habit as a masculine act. But today the emancipation of women has suppressed many of the feminine desires. More women now do the same work as men do. . . . Cigarettes, which are equated with men, become torches of freedom."

Brill's analysis, particularly his last statement, caught Bernay's imagination. "I found a way to help break the taboo against women smoking in public," he explained. "Why not a parade of women lighting torches of freedom—smoking cigarettes." Utilizing the feminist motif, and enlisting the support of "a leading feminist," Ruth Hale, Bernays had a contingent of cigarette-puffing women march in the 1929 Easter parade, down Fifth

Avenue in New York. "Our parade of ten young women lighting 'torches of freedom' on Fifth Avenue on Easter Sunday as a protest against woman's inequality caused a national stir," Bernays proclaimed. "Front-page stories in newspapers reported the freedom march in words and pictures."[83]

A "liberated" woman of the 1929 vintage appeared in ads such as this one for Hoover vacuum cleaners:

> I was the woman whose husband gave her each Christmas some pretty trinket. The woman whose youth was slipping away from her too fast. The woman whose cleaning burdens were too heavy. . . . In one short year I have discovered that youth need not go swiftly—that cleaning duties need not be burdensome. For last Christmas my husband did give me a *Hoover.*[84]

Other ads drew even more directly from libertarian language. Toastmaster proclaimed itself "The *Toaster* that FREED 465,000 HOMES. . . . From ever watching, turning or burning toast."[85]

Although according to the ideology of American business, the American woman was to remain identified with the home, it was a home whose definition had been severely altered by the explosion in production and distribution. No longer the repository of craft and self-sustaining values, the home of the 1920s saw the massive influx of industrial goods and values which made most of those crafts superfluous. Advertisers were quite conscious of the competition between new manufactured goods and older forms of home products and production. Their ads, they felt, must dramatize this competition and ceremonialize the victory of the new life style. *Printers' Ink,* the center of theory for the ad industry, turned often to such a task. The journal reinforced the need to substitute factory-made consumables for many of the products which had been produced traditionally as a part of women's activities. Speaking of the practice of bread baking in the home, *Printers' Ink* writer G. A. Nichols described it as the "greatest impediment to progress" that the biscuit industry confronted. The biscuit campaigns, he asserted, must utilize "antidote" methods, debunking bread baking, while at the same time "it will have to educate the people into using more biscuits."[86]

Other ads gave a slight twist to such a strategy. Rather than debunk the old ways outright, they offered the possibility of fusing old preferences and practices with new products. After telling how Fels-Naptha Soap made the boiling of clothes unnecessary, one ad gave ambivalent respect to the *old* way of doing things:

> Boil clothes with Fels-Naptha if you wish. Women have been used to boiling clothes for so long that to many it seems too good to be true that Fels-Naptha makes the dirt let go in water of any temperature.[87]

Here, while the soap certainly reduced the drudgery of housework, it also introduced an altered world view. Where wives in earlier families had held much "finger knowledge" about the right and wrong way of doing things, ads like this for Fels-Naptha reduced their knowledge to superstition. Old preferences appeared as "respected" but at the same time *useless* prejudices of a bygone era. Judgment and knowledge had been removed as all but a ceremonial or "fanciful" aspect of women's home activity.

While some, like Christine Frederick, heralded the entry of the machine-age into the home as a "household revolution" which freed women from toil,[88] the reduction in time for housework seems to have been elusive for many women. Despite the introduction of goods and machines which tended to routinize and take the "guess work" out of housework, sociologist Ruth Lindquist found, in her 1930 studies of the American family, that housework was still seen by most women as a general source of fatigue and worry. These women felt no more relieved than in the premechanized days of housetending. "It is something of a paradox," she observed, "that a deluge of labor-saving devices, new sources of power, more commercial agencies in the community and an actual decrease in the size of families have not prevented homemaking from being more than a full-time job."[89]

Rather than viewing the transformations in housework as *labor-saving*, it is perhaps more useful to view them as *labor-changing*. As industrial factories had transformed the broad nature of labor and production, so too had the influx of commercially produced household goods changed the nature of housework. "More than a few of the mothers" of *Middletown* complained that "their daughters, fresh from domestic science [home economics] in school, ridicule the mothers' inherited rule-of-thumb practices as 'old fashioned.'"[90] More and more, women were instructed that modern science, as a property of industrial corporations, should guide and define their motherly roles.

The transformation was well described by Christine Frederick, the ideologue of scientific home economy. In instructing manufacturers on the ways in which they should develop manuals and instructions for their wares, she emphasized that these manuals must serve the historic function of habituating women to new modes of production. Clearly elucidating the significance of women's adaptation to new commodities, she offered the following:

I affirm that the manufacturer's real success is measured by the degree of thoroughness with which the owner or operator of the appliance has been able to adapt herself to a transformation from a hand and craft technique over into a machine process.[91] (Emphasis in original.)

"Who is to train the woman out of the handcraft age, into a machine operative except the manufacturer?" she asked.

Women's work had traditionally been viewed as home-production, set apart from the world of industry. The entry of industrial goods into the home, however, tended to integrate the acceptable conception of *woman* with the conception of *worker* that prevailed in the factory. "The difficult role of wife," as Groves and Ogburn observed, had now been "brought more into harmony with the desires which social culture [industry] stimulates in the modern woman."[92] Though the home-centeredness of women still separated them from the external world of men, the industrially fabricated content of the home was defined and demarcated, more and more, by the external priorities of capitalism. The primacy of industrialism was making a captive anachronism out of the home-defined woman, while the predominant patriarchal ideal still sought to contain her within the traditional domain. Here lay a festering contradiction of modern womanhood, one which would emerge in years to come in a reinvigorated feminism.

As the housewife assumed more of a factory-operative status, the home became a place where the values of factory production, and the conditions if not the pay of the wage worker, were replicated and reinforced on a day-to-day basis. Such a development cannot be separated from the widespread increase in the employment of women in factories. Given the reserve nature of women's work, the "proletarianization" of housework was a way in which some of the tension between home and industry might be resolved.

As factory production had made work an integer within a vastly defined network of processes, the agencies of consumption made the wife a part of a corporately defined productive and distributive process. In a study of the woman as administrator of the modern home, Anna E. Richardson of the American Home Economics Association gave specificity to such a development. Writing in 1929, she declared that modern manufacturing had made it "impossible for the homemaker to have command of all the information demanded to buy intelligently." The divisions of labor which had made artisan crafts anachronistic, and separated the individual worker from a total sense of his/her product, now characterized the plight of house workers. The "wife" was merely a cog in a vastly corporatized process of production for the home. Her administrative role was seen within such a network:

> Retail business employs thousands of expert purchasing agents to select the goods which are sold to the home. . . . Modern methods of production make it impossible for the homemaker to know the quality of the materials which go into manufactured articles, and she has little assurance, except an occasional guarantee by a reputable manufacturer or retailer, that the article she buys will come up to any standard specification.

Richardson then continued to speak of how industrial propaganda further reinforced the proletarian status of modern womanhood. "Her problem is further complicated by advertising, which displays goods so attractively, that she is sometimes tempted to buy unwisely, without sufficient study of needs and how they can be met best. The psychology of clever advertising is frequently pitted against the common sense of the homemaker, with the result that she is worsted in the struggle."[93] The displacement of crafts, which Frederick had celebrated so enthusiastically, found women in a severe dilemma. The break from old drudgery had been integrated into a process whereby they were being divested of much knowledge and control of their work place.

American manufacturers presented housewives with a reconstructed ideal which gave much notice to their new identity as industrial workers. Throughout Frederick's work, for example, the ideology of the industrialized home is found. As the organization of the work processes of industry were increasingly defined by the assembly line and scientific management, Frederick "took over the principles one by one from the factory and applied them to the household."[94]

The industrialization of the home was a theme for others as well. In the late twenties, the Brooklyn Gas Company commissioned Lillian Gilbreth, who along with her husband Frank was one of the founders of time-motion study, to design a 10 × 12 foot kitchen "as an industrial production problem."[95] Siegfried Giedion, whose study of modern technology is brilliant and exhaustive, has further noted that the rational order of the Dining Car Galley served as an archetype for much kitchen design of the twenties.[96] The galley, which was designed for serving large numbers of people, was adapted to serve the nuclear family. The values of producing for the "mass" were being inculcated within the context of the modern home.

The task of training women away from handcrafts into the routines of machine operatives went beyond the "industrialization" of household technology and kitchen design. American women were forcing a far broader reorientation as they became increasingly employed outside as well as inside the home. To these new entrants into the labor force especially, machines offered a liberating potentiality that seemed essential. The feminists had demanded *socially useful toil* and an end to drudgery; others, concerned with the health of women, saw the ameliorative promise of the simplification of tasks. Abraham Myerson, a physician who treated women suffering from nervous exhaustion, spoke of the "need to break away from traditional cooking apparatus and traditional diet. The installation and use of fireless cookers, self-regulating ovens. . . . The discarding of most of the puddings, roasts, fancy dishes that take much time and preparation," he reasoned, would be of general benefit to women whose actual social role was increasingly defined beyond the scope of the nineteenth-century home.[97] Yet among manufacturers, the shift from handcraft to machine was not centered around the issue of women's departure from the home and their participation in industry, but was aimed rather at the reconstitution of traditionally conceived women's work in terms of current industrial exigencies. Noting that by 1929 more than 80 percent of the family's needs were satisfied by purchases by women, advertising people felt that it would be through women that new values of mass production might best be conveyed.[98]

While the culture tended to reinforce a conception of industry as a world of men, the distribution of mass-produced goods raised women to new significance in the mind of business. Their day-to-day activities were seen as integral to the sustenance of the productive system. "The wife's service" was becoming one of "directing the consumption by her selection of the goods and services" that the society was producing.[99]

Increasingly by the late twenties the consumption of goods was described by business as a creative and directive enterprise. At times, even academia reiterated this view. The American Academy of Political and Social Science, in a publication on the role of women in modern America (1929), concluded that mass consumption had made of the "modern housewife . . . less of a routine worker and more of an administrator and enterpriser in the *business of living.*" Women were depicted as the economic foremen of family life. Home craft, unlike other artisanship, had allegedly passed not into routine work, but into *self-determination.* Thus women could "work out an economic plan of life in which [family] . . . resources are utilized to buy the best possible combinations of satisfactions for today, and the best sequence of satisfactions for the future."[100] Such a sanguine view of socialized consumption was consistently mirrored in the ads' conception of women in the twenties. Women were the repository of choice and freedom that mass-marketed goods were said to encompass. Women were invested with a high degree of political and social determining power—a formation which linked the expanding commodity market with the political climate born out of suffrage.

Encouraging women to add Fleischmann's Yeast to their family diet (1922), one ad spoke of how "science has revolutionized the housewife's *ordering* of meals"— implicit agreement to a spectatorial partnership between industrial science and housewives as home "managers." Elsewhere, the managerial status of women was similarly ossified within a blind obedience to the scientific authority of the marketplace. Ads continually reaffirmed the necessary link between the new liberated female role and the new market. A 1929 ad for Bohnalite automobile pistons celebrated the modern woman's elevation:

> American women nowadays have a broad and clearer understanding of progress and achievement. Time was when things mechanical were out of their reach. But now Milady knows what is going on and why.
> The modern feminine drivers know all about this advanced piston.[101]

Women in the ads were invested with a wide control and knowledge—circumscribed, however, by the ideology of the consumer market. "Your husband may forget this," one ad for Mobil Arctic Oil cautioned women, "but you won't. You know that being careful [about auto maintenance] means more money for other things."[102] The image of woman had been widened to encompass a broad involvement in industry that went beyond the purely domestic sphere. She had become the home director, although her need for education in the broad categories of mass consumption was constantly emphasized to her.

Even in the area of motherhood, women were told to rely on the guidance provided by ads and other corporate agencies of information. Motherhood had become a profession sustained by industrial production. Women were warned of dangers in their homes, to their children, and told of commodity solutions. Hygeia baby bottles were "safe" and would not "carry germs to your baby." Fly-Tox bug killer was presented as the one line of defense for an otherwise "defenseless" child.[103]

Often the mystified tasks of motherhood involved inscrutable and even invisible aspects of home management. Mothers were told that the morbidly illustrated "gray spectre" that haunted children with skinned knees could be fought with Bauer & Black surgical dressings.[104] Women were instructed to follow the dictates of "health authorities" who "tell us that disease germs are everywhere." Lysol divided the house into an assemblage of minutely defined dangers, so mothers were told that they should be aware that even "the doorknobs threaten [children] . . . with disease."[105] Indeed family safety and survival were at stake for the mother who had become the buyer and dispenser of goods.

As women found their work worlds expanded to encompass both home and industry,[106] the ideological pressures of the consumer market mounted and the duties of the home became less productive and more passively received. While some students of modern life flattered the housewife into viewing "retail buying [as] . . . a productive act . . . [which could] multiply many fold the satisfactions from a given income," others viewed the contemporary woman more in terms of a functionary[107]—a bureaucrat of distribution, secondary to the husband whose wage made him the source of exchange, the source of survival. "Woman is . . . powerful in buying," Christine Frederick explained, "because of her *secondary* position to men." Despite the growing incidence of employed mothers, Frederick contended that a woman "is not a man's equal in earning and doing and building."

The patriarchal ideal had been adapted to the modern industrial system. Now the line of distinction between men and women was not drawn from their actual work reality, because both were significant factors in industrial production. Rather, it reinforced the *privatization* of consumption in a situation where production was increasingly *social*. It was a conception which reconciled the individualism of a wage process with the sociality of a factory system. Women, in Frederick's eyes, must gravitate toward an ideology which sustained the patriarchal home in a world in which many of its functions had become outmoded. Women, she argued, must accept "the position of quartermaster rather than general in the . . . *mutual organization* [of marriage.] She takes charge of the supplies largely for the very reason that she can't lead the forces in the field."[108] Although the husband was defined here as "general" because he brought in the wage, it was clear that the directive powers over the home were really invested in the hands of industry. It was equally clear that the woman's second-level decision-making capacity was only a euphemism for decisions made on the corporate level.

If consumption of mass-produced goods could be equated with free choice, then the direction of consumption could appear to be a new and liberated role. The modern housewife, Frederick proclaimed in her public lecture, "is no longer a cook—she is a can-opener." She doesn't prepare food, but dispenses it. In substitution for the productive knowledge of old, the modern housewife was to be educated into the facts and integers of modern life: she must "know her groceries" and "know her calories."[109] Women were encouraged to depend on the growing home-economics services for their managerial technique. Throughout the country, schools of homemaking either directly or indirectly conveyed the idea of a new approach to housework. In the twenties, schools like Pratt Institute (New York), Garland School and Fanny Farmer (Boston), and Lewis Institute (Chicago) flourished, reaching young women as they moved into adulthood. Along with these, high-school home economics, lectures, magazine contests, newspaper-sponsored schools, 4-H, and Home Bureau Demonstrations demarcated the emergence of the home as an object of broad social and often corporate concern.[110] In addition to the general areas of home management, subjects taught included, "care of hair, skin, and teeth, food preparation, home equipment and music for the home." By the mid-thirties, both General Electric (1932) and Westinghouse Electric (1934) had opened special cooking institutes which combined cooking instruction and the use of the all-electric kitchen they were interested in popularizing.[111]

This form of education provided yet another conduit for the flow of mass-produced goods to the domestic consumer.[112] Home production was shown to be antiquated. This was the ideological environment which informed the mothers in the 10 million new homes started between World War I and 1929, and which reached the "17,000,000 little girls" who were fourteen in 1920 and twenty-four at the close of the decade.

While the modern "Mom" was, through her general education, learning to habituate herself to the facts and premises of the marketplace, so too was she redefining her role as moral educator and socializer; this redefinition as well was to be adapted to the consumption process. The *Ladies' Home Journal*, by 1922, was offering a series of books on how to raise children: J. Morris Slemons, *The Prospective Mother*; L. Emmett Holt, *The Care and Feeding of Children*; Emelyn L. Coolidge, *The Home and Care of Sick Children*; and Miriam Finn Scott, *How to Know Your Child*. The last of these titles, dealing more with intuition than science, was, characteristically, the only one by a woman. These, like much of the other material in the *Journal*, unified the tasks of motherhood and consumption, even down to the purchasing of advice in these books.[113]

In a society unschooled in the ways of mass production and consumption, such information and implementation had been integral to a mother's girlhood upbringing. In a factory society which increasingly tore women's energies from the home, the commodified tips on how to raise children were a substitute. One working-class mother of *Middletown* expressed the feeling of many others when she spoke of her reliance on modern technologies and industrial culture for what would once have been her own responsibility. Explaining her dependency on the movies "as an aid in child-rearing," she said: "I send my daughter because a girl has to learn the ways of the world somehow and the movies are a good safe way."[114]

As industrial culture tended to ratify a separation of the ideological world of women (consumption) from that of men (production), both were defined by the same external agencies. As the culture identified men with work, the mother was maintained as the intra-family counselor or educator—a phenomenon which, according to Ruth Lindquist, made "excessive demands . . . upon the mother."[115] Faced with the unhappy prospect of culturally identifying herself in the isolation of the home, along with the increasing reality of work outside the home, mothers of the twenties were prime targets for ads which offered corporate aid in the problems of child rearing. Often appealing to women's guilt over not being able to devote all the time necessary to take care of children, the ads reached out to both the needs and the fears of mothers. Suggesting that Grape-Nuts can create sound adults out of endangered children, a testimonial from an unnamed "famous scientist" ominously told mothers to "Tell me what your children eat and I will show you the kind of men and women they will be!"[116]

Such ads played on the inadequacy that mothers must have felt, compelled as they were to look outside the home for survival, yet burdened with a continued responsibility to raise children "right." Through consumption, the ads argued, the broad crisis of mothers in industrial America could be resolved. The educational input of ads was that by using certain products on children, and by educating them into certain patterns of consumption, their futures would be ensured. In such ads, the traditional expectations of womanhood were combined with the notion that only through children, through youth, could cultural stability be achieved. As consumers, women could meet the cultural expectations of motherhood, and perhaps even raise their children to be better consumers than they themselves were.

It was through their children that parents might experience the possible benefits of modern life. An ad in the *Ladies' Home Journal* pictured a mother watching her daughter at the piano:

> FOR HER . . . All the things you wanted . . . everything you hoped to be. Old hopes, old ambitions . . . how they come alive again now! Talents that somehow or other you neglected . . . opportunities you let slip by. . . . How eagerly you hope it might be different with her.[117]

Such ads clearly fused the traditional image of the mother as socializer with feelings drawn from the feminist critique of that role. Following the pattern of advertising policy in general, the above ad identified itself with an implicit critique of the cultural milieu reinforced by industrial society. It encouraged women to educate their children and live through them at the same time. It shared the world view of working-class housewives who espoused the following aspirations for their female progeny: "I've always wanted my girls to do something other than housework; I don't want *them* to be house drudges like me!"[118] The promise of the new corporate authority was an end to the trap which patriarchy had traditionally posed for women. Where the patriarchal structure had required the socialization of young girls into an acceptance of drudgery as destiny, the vision of the future of the commodity market dangled before women's eyes resembled that which the feminists among them were already seeing as a possibility: a society in which the patriarchal yoke might be broken and in which women might expect their daughters' lives to transcend the historic limitations of their own.

The tension between the continued ideal of motherhood and the growing inadequacy of that role served as fertile ground for indicating an advertised and consumerized escape. While women within the ads were still caught in the role of motherhood, consumption was linked to their educative function to imply a way for their daughters to do better. Through consumption, women could procure for their children the kind of life-long security and happiness that was associated with perpetual youth. Protecting and educating children was tantamount to training them from infancy in beneficial patterns of consumption. J. B. Watson's emphasis on creating new forms of behavior through youth found its propagandistic realization. Colgate's Dental Cream pictured a beautiful young woman, clearly viable on the sexuo-economic marketplace, embracing her child. Explaining that this mother had captured youth by beginning to use Colgate in 1908, the ad implied that an early introduction of training into beauty, and more importantly into consumption, was essential to the child. After brushing her own way to youthful beauty, "now her Daughter uses the same dental cream."[119] Another ad was more explicit as to what socialization meant. Depicting a mother and infant daughter, the ad implored, "From her very first smile" use Palmolive Soap. "Correct skin-care starts in infancy. It is a duty that every mother owes her child." The rewards for adopting such an educational philosophy were in tune with the demands of the age. "'School-girl Complexions' come now as a natural result. . . . To assure your child's having one through the years, you must take proper steps now."[120]

7 Consumption and Seduction

As women were encouraged to accept a self-definition of home manager, their corporately defined role also required that they continually manage and define themselves. Within the widespread association of women and the home, the modern housewife remained wageless in her capacity of "quartermaster." Operating in what she was told was her "proper" place, she was encouraged to maintain a barter system of sorts to ensure her livelihood. While the skills of her mother and grandmother had been productive, her own were increasingly depicted as tricks of the flesh.

The women in ads were constantly observing themselves, ever self-critical. Throughout the twenties, a noticeable proportion of magazine ads directed at women depicted them looking into mirrors.[121] Even in the midst of efficient home management women were reminded that it was their appearance more than their organizational capacities which would ensure fidelity in particular and home security in general. Just as men were encouraged to cultivate their appearance to impress the boss, for women the imperative of beauty was directly linked to the question of job security—their *survival*, in fact, depended upon their ability to keep a husband, ads continually reminded women—or more precisely, the wage that he brought home to underwrite their managerial role. In one ad for a highly mechanized and rationalized Boone kitchen cabinet (replete with coffee mill, swinging stool, card index, daily reminder, timer-clock, disappearing ironing board, knife sharpener and bread board) women were assured that central to this kitchen work-place was a "mirror—for that hasty glance." It was taken for granted that personal appearance was a central category of their job.[122]

Just as the modern woman was expected to spend the family income in making the home, sociologists Groves and Ogburn noted that she also had to "decide how to spend her personality . . . to bring the family and herself the greatest quantity of satisfactions."[123] Her personality and looks were integrated into her other multifarious commodified skills of survival and were posed as the way to vie in a world where her concrete productive capacities had nearly evaporated, and where "keen and critical" glances constantly threatened her. As her homemaking skills had been reconstituted into a process of accumulating mass-produced possessions, her sexuo-economic capacities were reinforced on a commercial plane. An ad for Woodbury Soap (1922) offered women "the possession of a beautiful skin" which might arm them to meet a hostile world "proudly — confidently — without fear."[124] Another Woodbury ad warned women that "a man expects to find daintiness, charm, refinement in the woman he knows," and that in order to maintain his pleasure, a woman must constantly spend on her appearance. The ad went so far as to warn, "And when some unpleasant little detail mars this conception of what a woman should be—nothing quite effaces his involuntary disappointment."[125] Another ad suggested that life-long marriage and security were "beauty's reward" and might be effected by using Pompeian Night Cream.[126]

The real insecurity women felt about "what a woman should be" is clearly manipulated in these ads of the twenties. As woman's social role became increasingly defined in terms of consumption—a job which required no more than an obedience to the dictates of the marketplace—the core of the modern housewife's success lay in her ability to charm and bewitch. Naturally here too, industry played an indispensable role. As one ad for Madame Surilla Perfume noted, "very often the subtlety of an exquisity odeur, and not the lady herself, does the befuddling."[127] From the field of social psychology, advertising had borrowed the notion of the *social self* as a prime weapon in its arsenal. Here people defined themselves in terms set by the approval or disapproval of others. In its particular economic definition of womanhood, consumer ideology relied heavily on this notion.

In the middle of her mechanically engineered kitchen, the modern housewife was expected to be overcome with the issue of whether her "self," her body, her personality were viable in the socio-sexual market that defined her job. Ads of the 1920s were quite explicit about this narcissistic imperative. They unabashedly used pictures of veiled nudes and women in auto-erotic stances to encourage self-comparison and to remind women of the primacy of their sexuality. A booklet advertising feminine beauty aids had on its cover a picture of a highly scrubbed, powdered and decorated nude. The message of the title was explicit: "Your

Masterpiece—Yourself." Women were being educated to look at themselves as things to be created competitively against other women: painted and sculpted with the aids of the modern market.[128]

Carl B. Naether, an ad man whose contributions included the most widely-read study of the twenties on how to advertise to women, encouraged the implementation of such tactics in advertising. Using an ad for pearls as an example, Naether discussed the message that the picture conveyed. The illustration showed a woman wearing a breast-length strand of pearls. With one hand she fondled her bosom. According to Naether, this represented an effective way of making women self-conscious about their bodies and of directing this self-consciousness toward consumption. "They [the pearls] center attention on those parts of the feminine body which they encircle and touch," he explained. "Thus," he continued, the ad "ingeniously compares women with these precious adornments, attributing to the former the qualities possessed by the latter." Locating female beauty in the realm of consumable objects, Naether argued, the ad would elicit "feelings of vanity and pride," which were central to the sexually competitive nature of the modern woman.[129] Sensuality had been reformulated into something resembling the cash nexus.

Even women well into motherhood were assured by advertisers that they might maintain the kind of youthful beauty that would guarantee their social security. H. W. Gossard Corsets could preserve "that line of beauty which girlhood claims as its own—that curve which Hogarth the artist pronounces the most beautiful in all creation . . . that line which, curving in gently at the waist, sweeps in graceful rhythm over the hip and down kneeward." Ads like this one used romantic and literary prose to simulate a seduction, suggesting to women that as they were being productively displaced by the marvels of the machine age, they might rely on their trump card, aesthetic supremacy. Thus a Gossard Corset might secure for women, who had undergone both childbirth and years of housekeeping, a body which would maintain Hogarth's raptures: a "line which makes woman's form the most perfect on earth."[130]

The pursuit of beauty through consumption was numbered among the modern skills of survival for women. While married women in fact entered the labor market with increasing frequency, the dominant ideology told them to look homeward for their proper role. Thus there was a tension between women as wage earners and the ideal of *woman* which was essentially wageless. Separating men from women around the issue of who should bring in the wage, the advertising ideology brought them together through commodity-based sexuality. This was where the wage process was reconciled with a home which still sustained itself on a barter system.

Still bound to a patriarchal yoke, American women faced a level of insecurity which made ads for youth, beauty and sensuality an effective and meaningful part of their environment. Marketing research of the twenties seems to bear this out. One survey, done in small Midwestern towns where wives were likely to be actually home-bound while husbands brought in a wage, reflects the receptivity toward ads. Performed in nine towns in Kansas, Missouri, Nebraska, and Iowa, the survey showed that in 1926 a great majority of women said that they paid a "good" or "great deal" of attention to advertising. Their predilection was strongly in favor of the national ads seen in magazines over the local ads of newspapers.[131] Divested of survival capacities of her own, advertising's woman relied on commodities to secure a social bond with a family which was losing its productive intrarelationship.

For the modern woman the alleged managerial responsibility of consumption had little objective content, and the survival tactic of allurement became appended to it as the most conspicuous form of self-definition. Now even mothers must rely on Palmolive Soap's school-girl skin in order to ensure the support of the entire family, children included. One ad, with Oedipal implications, showed a beautiful young mother submitting to her boy-child's scrutiny and pleasure. Through the use of Palmolive, women were told, they could maintain themselves as "His first Love."[132] As ads documented the transition from the productive-knowledge of traditional home activity to the discipline of industrial capitalism, women's creative roles were increasingly displaced. The advertised duties of the *wife* became intertwined with the last home industry—marital sex.

> Woman's deep-seated instinct urging her to the use of perfumes is a manifestation of a fundamental law of biology. *The first duty of woman is to attract.* . . . It does not matter how clever or independent you may be, if you fail to influence the men you meet, consciously or unconsciously, you are not fulfilling your fundamental duty as a woman. . . .[133]

Despite the managerial lingo which had come to be applied to womanhood, the inadequacy and insecurity of such an "industrialized" role was reflected in the overbearing call for sexual skills. If consumption management was a *role* of work, sexuality was, for women, a *duty* of leisure. The two, work and leisure, could not be separated. Consumption provided an idiom for the unity of the two.

The crisis in the family had been an ongoing experience since the beginnings of industrialism, sorely felt in the period of the 1920s just as it is today. For some, particularly among socialists and feminists, the transition from a family or community based mode of production indicated a potential liberation from the oppressions of patriarchal authority. On two critical levels, the birth of industrialism gave underpinnings to such hope. First, the industrialization of production pointed to an end to scarcity. The possibility of abundance was raised as the consolidation of human and material resources integrated productive energies which for many promised to bring an end to chronically unfulfilled needs. Second, the extrication of questions of survival from the context of patriarchally controlled bonds of kinship, and particularly relations between men and women, meant the beginnings of a concept of society divested of its traditionally authoritarian character.

While many Americans of the 1920s held fast to social forms which were becoming less viable, futuristic thought perceived the coming of an age in which new social bonds would arise, cemented by affection and emotional interdependence rather than by the dictates of traditional patriarchy. Yet such positive visions of the future as those contained in the thought of Floyd Dell and Charlotte Perkins Gilman offered little solace to those who felt the time and space of their lives increasingly penetrated, not freed, by the dictates of *new* industrial authorities. Posed against the libertarian potential of industrial society were the disciplinary instincts of those who held the controls over production.

In the death of patriarchy, both libertarians and business shared an interest. Yet their interests were at odds with one another. To Dell, the machine age would be the era of romantic love, sexuality freed from the obligations of necessity. To American business, the romantic, antipatriarchal attitude was a vital tool for replacing the social authority of kinship taboos with the social authority of corporate enterprise.

Within the vision of the nuclear, or perhaps more precisely the *atomic* family, the ideologues of mass consumption tried to effect a synthesis between the socially felt need for human relationships and the economic imperative of breaking down all traditional social bonds in favor of the bonds generated by the productive apparatus. The new family was a parody of the old. There was Mom, Dad and the Kids. Yet the link between them was thoroughly externalized through their common involvement within the time-space dictates of business. The roles of the father and mother, the concept of romance and the erotic facet of sexuality were now defined by their common, corporate source. If parents objected to this transformed authority, it was through their children—depicted as total consumers— that the ad men and consumption ideologues hoped to appropriate the future.

The commodified answers to the question of "how to live" began to take on a distinct character. Utilizing the collective image of the family, the ads in their contribution to mass culture did their best to deny that collectivity. For each aspect of the family *collective*—the source of decision making, the locus of child rearing, the things which elicited affectionate response—all of these now pointed outward toward the world of commodities for their direction. Corporate America had begun to define itself as *the father of us all.*

Consumer Report:
The Social Crisis of the Mass Culture

From the vantage point of the 1970s, consumerism no longer represents a changing capitalist social order; it has become an idiom of daily life with a matter-of-fact status within American culture. While advertising still offers its own version of social amelioration, Americans have increasingly questioned the ability of the marketplace to work out social and personal problems. At the same time, however, the commodity system enjoys a kind of passively accepted legitimacy as the universal arena within which most human needs are to be met in the United States. Even Vance Packard, who has been a leading critic of mass culture in America, emerges as a strong proponent of this legitimacy. Accepting advertising or, more broadly, the massive apparati of cultural "divertissement," as second nature to modern life, Packard's analysis itself has been neutralized by its fixation on questions of *corruption* and *abuse*. Viewing the authoritarian tendencies within modern commercial culture as nonessential nuances, Packard's scathing criticism founders on the question of the *ultimate value* of advertising in the modern era. In prefacing his widely read book on motivational techniques in advertising (*The Hidden Persuaders*, 1957), Packard notes that all that he will divulge about capitalism is on some level *eccentric* rather than *systemic*. While attacking the implantation of motivational research into the crevices of our lives, Packard separates these "subterranean" operations (covert) out from their legitimate (overt) co-conspiracies:

> Since our concern here is with the breed of persuaders known in the trade as the "depth boys," much of the book is devoted to describing their subterranean operations. For that reason I should add the obvious: a great many advertising men, publicists, fund raisers, personnel experts, and political leaders, in fact numerically a majority, still do a straightforward job and accept us as rational citizens (whether we are or not). They fill an important and constructive role in our society. Advertising, for example, not only plays a vital role in promoting our economic growth but is a colorful, diverting aspect of American life; and many of the creations of ad men are tasteful, honest works of artistry.[1]

Perhaps such a disclaimer seemed reasonable in the context of the 1950s. Today it clearly misses the point. Whether or not the advertising industry has become the mainstay of artistry in American life is not the issue. *Why* and *how* and to *whose benefit* seems a more productive line of questioning. Also, the question of whether or not commerce has become the source for diversion and growth seems less explosive than the question of *how* this has happened (the corporate mobilization of networks of communications, work, transportation, community, etc.) and what it points to regarding the need for fundamental social changes.

If one goes to the beginnings of the modern consumer culture in the twenties, the inadequacy of a perspective such as Vance Packard's comes clear. To chastise the abuses of a structure which depends on abuse is off the mark. As we look at the social roots of the modern consumer culture in preceding sections, we can perceive it as something other than the unquestioned social "given" that it purports to be. Rather, we see it born as an apparatus for doing battle for the control of social space. It was born and continues in contestation for control over daily life. Each time that the Coca-Cola Bottling Company informs us that their product is "The Real Thing©", implicit is the message that it isn't the real thing after all; and what is more, people do feel the need for the actual real thing. To the extent that an ad, or the corporate interest that it represents, speaks for something meaningful, it does so within a context of extreme tension. There are wishes and needs which are generated in spite of the marketplace, yet the marketplace purports to address them. In a Coke ad, there is the understanding that the demand and struggle for something *real* will be diverted, defined as subversive or folly, and that "The Real Thing©" will serve as an acceptable embodiment of the impulse for something more real, more gratifying.

This ideological motif began to emerge during the 1920s, which was a time rife with social conflict. The consumer culture grew in response to that crisis and to the monumental growth of productive capacity with which it was interlaced. As production changed and as the social character of work became even more routinized and monotonous, the consumer culture presented itself as the realm within which gratification and excitement might be had—an alternative to more radical and anti-authoritarian prescriptions. As the social life and bonding patterns of the traditional family became a ground for upheaval and feminism, the marketplace attempted to sell capitalism as a social mode within which meaningful relationships might be constituted. As immigration and the migration of a domestic population from an agrarian into an industrial context precipitated a cultural shock from the very beginnings of American industrial capitalism, the consumer culture of the twenties responded with definitions of *Americanization* and *modernization* which aspired to mollify social conflict. The aim was the consolidation of a new "national character" keyed to the exigencies of expanding capitalism. On each level, the amelioratives of the marketplace were ongoing alternatives posed against anticapitalist tendencies, against the principle of people determining the terms of their own existence. On every level, obedience was posited favorably against self-direction; an obedience clothed in utopian imagery.

The rise of advertising and consumerism in the twenties was part of a broader change in the character of capitalist society. Commercial propaganda didn't act as the determinant of change, but was in many ways *both* a reflection and agent of transformation. Advertising raised the banner of consumable social democracy in a world where monumental corporate development was eclipsing and redefining much of the space in which critical alternatives might be effectively developed. As it became the voice of American mass-produced and consumed culture, it did so within a context of shrinking arenas for popularly defined culture.

While the contours of commercial culture were taking on a decided modernity by the 1920s, it was decades before the commodified "good life" took hold to the degree only dreamed of in the twenties. In the period between 1920 and the end of the Second World War, American capitalism's ability to expand markets commensurate with its growing productive capacity was severely limited. In the twenties, and even more so during the Depression, high levels of production were plagued by the rationale of profitability, by the dominant mode of distribution. In the tension between what was profitable and what people needed, profitability won out.

In the name of reconsolidating markets, the ideologies of the thirties harkened to a frontier vision of committed sacrifice more than to immediate gratifications. With the entry of the U.S. into World War II, however, things began to change. War industries created jobs and reinvigorated domestic markets. Postwar policies were a further step toward reconciling consumerism and social order. After the war, the war industries remained mobilized, expanding in the shadow of a new—albeit "cold"—war. Military ventures into Korea and Indochina provided an integral *raison d'être* for the maintenance of this sector of the economy. The policies of the United States in Western Europe (e.g., the Marshall Plan) further created a climate in which high levels of productivity could be absorbed and maintained by "new markets" for military, capital and consumer goods.

It was in the period of postwar boom that the social policies postulated and initiated in the twenties began to make their most effective inroads upon the social landscape of American society. During this period of broad commercialism and suburbanization, the idea of a *free world* characterized by *goods* established itself as a pacific social ethic. Yet even then, in the "good times" of the fifties, social discontent remained. Coincident with the pacified imagery of suburban life stood a more traditional and compulsory ethic to enforce it: the strict rule of conformity maintained by the patriotic imperatives of anti-communism, the cold war, and McCarthyism.

It is a big jump from the twenties to more recent

times. However, we should work toward a historical understanding of the implications of mass consumption. As the consumer society has taken form, and as its social costs become increasingly evident, the need for an analysis which goes beyond its corruptions, *to its root*, becomes central to the task of significant social change.

"The 'twentieth century,'" argued Arnold Hauser in his study, *The Social History of Art*, "begins after the first world war, that is to say, in the 'twenties,' just as the 'nineteenth century' did not begin until about 1830."[2] Concerning the rise of industrial capitalism and of factory production, Hauser's contention about the "nineteenth century" is convincing. At times the standard periodization-by-century doesn't make any sense. Likewise, if the configuration of our current epoch might best be understood in the spread of the corporate order, the bureaucratization of social institutions, the rise of decisive resistance to an expanding capitalism, and the emergence of *mass culture* to displace earlier forms, the 1920s was certainly a time when such developments began to coalesce.

Giving theoretical contours to Kafka's depiction of the modern world as one in which the irrational had become *rational*, many have observed that the twentieth century—particularly World War I onward—represents a critical break from earlier times. The particularities of twentieth-century developments have made a deep imprint upon the work of critics and analysts of capitalist society. The 1920s emerge as a watershed, the beginnings of a new social order codified by corporate developments. For some, the rise of this new order is best represented in the development of facism. In studying the rise of American corporate culture, however, certain broad developments within capitalist societies seem more relevant than an immediate comparison to Italy or Germany.

Georg Lukács, the Hungarian author of *History and Class Consciousness,* saw the regimentation of the capitalist order as having a decisive effect on the paradigms of work, social life and consciousness. Twentieth-century capitalism had entered a period in which all spheres of existence were informed by industry; the commodity had become a universal form. The very *perceptions* engendered within this process, argued Lukács, begin to reflect the priorities of capitalism: the primacy of the system of exchange, the destruction of craft, the fragmentation of work and social life. For Lukács, the notion of *time* itself had become identical to the spatial terms of the commodity world—relegating the notion of *what is* to the reified immortality of a "universal." *Time* was now circumscribed by the priorities of getting things done within the industrialized world of work and by the consumption of capitalism's goods and services for moments of leisure. Self-generated activity, outside of the contours of industrial capitalism and not yet merchandised by the various "leisure" industries, had become relegated to the dismissal, "doing nothing."

In Germany, and later in exile in the United States, the works of the Frankfurt School, Herbert Marcuse, Theodore Adorno, Max Horkheimer and others, reflected a concern with the canonization of the corporate order and a perception of the degree to which modern industrial society has penetrated the realms of social existence, molding them with the cold die of *rationality.*

Similarly, Harry Braverman, in his recent book, *Labor and Monopoly Capital,* tells of how the characteristic of the modern era has been the "degradation" of labor. Work, once a repository of skill and social interaction, has become a series of preordained gestures. The power of know-how has become firmly implanted in the *safe* confines of management, while obedience has become the most desired category that industry expects of its workers. Along with the degradation of labor in the industrial world, Braverman indicates that many of the interactions of the society have been similarly rationalized within service industries, governed by the same safe managerial principle. Martin Sklar, a founder of the American New Left, has given a more "economic" underpinning to much of what Braverman says. Sklar indicates that the creation of a new work format not only changes the labor process, but has broad implications as a way in which surplus capital may be profitably invested in areas which are less likely to be affected by the traditional scourge of overproduction: service industries and the development and bureaucratization of the state apparatus.

Within each of these analyses, the question of capitalist *culture* looms large. Each of the developments cited indicates the closing down of traditional arenas of social interaction and the expansion of the corporate principle into the details of people's lives.[3]

In the United States, some distinct characteristics of modern capitalism preceded the twenties. In the years immediately following 1900, corporate and governmental agencies became increasingly concerned with creating a rational social order, and these groups along with more genuinely humanistic reform elements began to come together in a broad social movement known in our history books as *Progressivism*. Along with the impulse toward a rational society, came the specific application of such an ideal to the production of goods. Industry, utilizing the techniques of time-motion experts like Frederick W. Taylor and Frank and Lilian Gilbreth, began to deploy "scientific management," a system designed to further the trend toward an orderly industrial schema. Scientific managers attempted to increase productivity by shifting the productive know-how away from working people and toward the hegemonic reliability of managerial planning and rationalized technology.

Yet while such techniques attempted to systematize production and neutralize conflict, they created a social unrest among the working population that further drove home the need for a corporate management which would direct the social world itself. The rationalization of modern industrial management became irreconcilably intertwined with the rising need for "scientific" techniques which could be applied to social management. It is no coincidence that the moment in question gave rise to a proliferating profession of social scientists working in the field and theorizing solutions in journals like the *Annals* of the American Association of Political and Social Science and the *Journal of Applied Psychology*. The implementation of "scientifically" calibrated monotony on the job required the development of a new science to deal with its effect on consciousness and social order.

At the other end of the spectrum, the response of workers and organized labor to rationalized "scientific" production had been sharp and damning. Citing "scientific management" as an assault on the "one great asset of the wage worker . . . his craftsmanship," laborers experienced new forms of production as an encroachment upon and the obliteration of the social culture of work.[4] For members of the Industrial Workers of the World (IWW), the "dequalification" (their term for removal of skill and know-how) of workers in the productive process was an act of war against them, an invitation for countermeasures of sabotage, passive resistance and syndicalism.[5]

Robert Franklin Hoxie, in *Scientific Management and Labor* (1921), further enumerated "the trade union objections to 'scientific management.'" Among labor's objections were the contentions that "'Scientific management' is opposed to industrial democracy; it is a reversion to industrial autocracy. It forces the workers to depend upon the employers' conception of fairness, and limits the democratic safeguards of the workers."

He continued, "'Scientific management,' in its relations to labor, is unscientific. . . . It violates the fundamental principles of human nature by ignoring temperament and habits." The issue of human need, personal and social, was integral to the attack.

"'Scientific management' tends to gather up and transfer to the management all the traditional knowledge, the judgment and the skill, and monopolizes the initiative of the worker in connection with the work.

"[Scientific management] enable[s] the employer to deal with workers as individuals, and thus to substitute individual for collective bargaining. . . . To pit workman against workman."[6]

In each angry objection stood the conviction that modern production, despite its claims to progress, was encroaching upon the space and autonomy of the working population. The period leading up to the twenties gave testimony to that conviction. Capping a period of intensive industrial violence, by 1919 a strike wave had become epidemic; the violations of modern management and the issues of autonomy over social space were at its core. Over the next decade, the advertising industry and commercial culture attempted to meet and defuse this widespread critique of modern industrial life.

The Russian Revolution, in 1917, had also signaled the arrival of the modern era. A historic shock felt throughout the capitalist world, the revolution caused industrialists grave concern; it further indicated a necessary *social* path for twentieth-century corporate development. With further anticapitalist revolution on the horizon (in Germany and Hungary), and with many immigrant workers bearing more than a coincidental connection to European movements, it was seen as necessary to meet the challenge not merely with direct force, but also with a change in the social and cultural dimensions of industrial life. Commensurate with the widespread demand for industrial democracy within working-class communities, corporate strategies addressed the need to undermine the subversive potential that these communities held. A concrete example of Lukács' observation about the universalization of the commodity, the commercial culture of the twenties draped itself with "social democratic" ideals, channeled toward the maintenance of capitalist power. The commercial culture strove to leave corporate domination of the productive process intact and at the same time speak to the demand for a richer social life for those who worked and lived within the industrial context.

By the end of the First World War, and indeed fertilized in its bloody and mechanized presence, the terms of modern capitalism had been set. In the 1920s, with the development of consumerism, advertising, and the growing utilization of mass communications on the national level, the American corporate order began to shape and publicize an affirmative social image for itself. The corporate message of the twenties was loud and clear. *Modern times* had arrived, defined largely by the burgeoning expanses of mass production, and addressing the "new freedoms" posed by the modern marketplace. Soon the commodity structure would engulf and displace modes of communication, patterns of family life, social mores and communitarian bonds which had belonged to an era now seen as decrepit and antiquated. The social channels of the marketplace and the culture that the marketplace generated were posed as beneficial correlaries to the less appealing aspects of modernity: the monotony of work, the decay of traditional social arenas, the political repression that was encountered by those who stuck to the "inappropriate" belligerency of working-class politics.

The corporate ideology of the twenties contended that the consumer society would meet and neutralize the political opposition to capitalism. Utilizing the promise of material well-being, conscripting the notion of industrial democracy, capitalizing on the degeneration of traditional and localized authorities, corporate America associated itself with the tasks of the most critical forces within the society—its opposition—while at the same time attempting to tame those forces.

During the nineteenth and early twentieth centuries, the industrial definition of social time and space stood at the core of social unrest. Industrial production had imposed a new ordering of time on the work process, as social space was increasingly circumscribed by the wage system and the broad imperatives of mechanical reproduction. As the issues of autonomy and self-determination rose to the fore in a chronically *managed* environment, it became necessary for corporate structures and ideologies correspondingly to address and embrace the popular call for a better life. Within mass consumption, advertising, and ultimately within the emergence of a *mass culture*, the tension between the socially expressed needs for self-defined time and space and the time-space dicta of corporation capitalism (long at odds with one another) began to be reconciled within the spirit of industrial management. A 1920s ad for Alpine Sun Lamps provides a provocative example. There are two illustrations in the ad. In the upper-right-hand corner there is an etching of a nude woman, arms outstretched, facing into the sun. The main illustration (at the center of the ad) depicts a woman lounging on the edge of her bathtub, robe open, her nakedness revealed, fondled and nurtured by the "vitally interesting message" of her Alpine Sun Lamp. The text of the ad reads as follows:

> If you were free to live . . . Were you today to throw off the restraints of social conformity . . . would you, too, first satisfy that inborn craving for Ultraviolet? Would you discard the trappings of civilization to spend strenuous health-brimmed days in the beneficent sunlight?
>
> For most convention-ridden people such action is denied. But the vital Ultraviolet portion of the sunlight can be brought right into the home by means of the justly famous *Alpine Sun Lamp*.[7]

The realities of urban industrialism had raised the issues of health, fresh air and inadequate space. Such critiques were not generated by the desire for sun lamps, but rather by more general and fundamental realities of the industrial context. Here in the Alpine ad, however, the critique reappears, along with a Freudian appeal to precivilized (*id*) urges, yet safely confined within the logical boundaries of the marketing process. Advertising, today, whether it sells cars as dream machines for country jaunts or "natural" cereals as a means for transcending the admitted evils of chemically fortified supermarket fare, maintains the same logic—the sense that a product contains the negation of its own corporate origins.

Advertising and much of what is generally termed

"mass culture" represent a deformed and internally contradicted corporate acceptance of that which power structures have historically forbidden. In a century in which political, social and sensual realms have been exploded by revolutionary resistance, the "mass culture" is a symbolic aquiescence, by capitalism, to what Freud termed the "return of the repressed." Western civilization in general and capitalist society in particular have maintained their guards on the political and social frontiers of freedom, yet the significance of the "mass culture" has often been an offering of "escape" from these controls and from the material immiserization and restricted sensual life that they have entailed. It is not uncommon for advertising to depict an exchange process which, despite its concrete limitations, contains the mortar of gratification. The linking of the marketplace to utopian ideals, to political and social freedom, to material well-being, and to the realization of fantasy, represents the spectacle of liberation emanating from the bowels of domination and denial.

Through the reproduction of social relations, and by redefining the landscape of freedom on and off the job, the American corporate structure has worked to achieve a social stability which eluded its control before the twenties and which has, at times, broken down in the years since.

During the nineteenth century, capitalist society had drawn its vitality from the innovations in productivity, accumulation and expansion. For working populations, this had meant an enforced ideology of hard work, thrift and sobriety—deferred if not denied gratification. Such disciplines, particularly as the rhythms of time-managed industry were imposed, stood at the core of discontent, generating a critique of industry as dehumanizing and industrialists as criminals. Socialism, syndicalism, anarchism and feminism emerged as industrial movements which sought to put industry in the hands of those who worked it; to turn industrial production toward meeting the needs of the working population. Realizing the utopian possibility held by a machinery which could mass-produce goods and the repressive reality that contained that machinery, these radicals called for a fundamental change in social relationships. Implicit within a variety of radical tendencies was the notion that industrial society contained a liberating potential, a potential submerged and diverted by those who currently authorized and profited from it.

Ironically, it was within these critical, often anticapitalist perspectives that capitalism began to discover the building blocks with which to erect its own affirmative social imagery. We must not take lightly the assertion heard among businessmen of the twenties that in mass production and mass consumption lay the answer to the gnawing threat of what was shorthandedly termed "bolshevism." In the corporate ideology of the 1920s, the goods of the marketplace were sold to the public with the "liberating" and "democratic" lingo which had up till then been heard most loudly among those whose attack was on the corporate premise of the market economy itself. Now, enfranchisement was linked to the increased capacity to produce and the concomitant need for national distribution of goods. Denying complicity in the deprivations of an *earlier* period of capitalist development, modern corporate propaganda began to internalize the critique of scarcity while at the same time attempting to obliterate the class dimensions of that critique. Corporate capitalism hoped to profit by the attack on its own failures.

In addition, as the rise of capitalism had put traditional family life into disarray, it also joined in on the feminist argument that patriarchal society was antiquated and oppressive. Since feminism had located the historic oppression of women within the patriarchal structure of the family, the corporate ideal of the twenties also took issue with the authority of the father. Yet while feminism had looked toward a world in which women would appropriate control over their own lives, the corporate debunking of the patriarchy coincided with a general devaluation of all forms of self-direction. In hailing the *modern woman* as a "home manager" and in celebrating the child as the conscience for a new age, corporate ideologues asserted that each was expected to devote a high degree of obedience to the directives of the consumer market. The industrial elevation of women and children served to relegate the traditional patriarch to an antedeluvian, sometimes comic characterization. Here mass culture shared the radical hopes for autonomy and equality. Yet once again, in its depiction of the modern family, the world of mass consumption faltered before the edge of change; as the father of old was relegated to the "dust bin of history," the corporate patriarch was crowned as a just and beneficent authority for a modern age.

During the 1920s the stage was set by which the expanding diversity of corporate organization might do cultural battle with a population which was in need of, and demanding, social change. The stage was in the theatre of daily life, and it was within the intimacies of that reality—productive, cultural, social, psychological—that a corporate *pièce-de-théâtre* was being scripted.

By the end of the twenties, the corporate generals and the captains of consciousness had made significant inroads into America's social territories. Brand names had inserted themselves into the idiom of daily expression, prepackaged foodstuffs were increasingly the culinary fare of the population, the automobile—perhaps the archetypal commodity—was no longer merely an idiosyncratic mode of transport but an artifact of multidimensional significance within the culture. Housing, also, was designed to underwrite monumental changes in the relationship between commerce and society. The embellishment of public schooling with modern "home economics" curricula is but one example of the way in which a mode of existence produced in industrial plants and publicized by advertising was being woven into the web of daily life.

Yet in many ways, the idea that consumerism was a means to social pacification and management remained a utopian dream in the minds of corporate theoreticians. Despite the attempts to maintain social order on a variety of levels, the deprivations and tensions of corporate industrial society were still experienced repressively by a wide sector of the population. The "Red Scare" of the early twenties maintained itself as a policy against radical opponents of the system. Also, the crises experienced within the realm of the family continued to be exposed, as they are today. While advertising attempted to forge a route to stability, it also pointed to a pervasive instability which festered within the society: the loss of productive skills, the family in crisis, widespread immiserization and economic insecurity, the sense that community bonds were weakening. The attempt to obliterate traditional cultures; the attempt to domesticate the social demands of working people within the realm of a consumption-oriented social democracy; the attempt to obscure the work place and to create a cultural vision which avoided the question of the capitalist organization of work; the attempt to reconsolidate and supplant family life—all of these efforts spoke to the myriad of tensions within the society of the twenties. Each strategy betrayed the dialectical resistance which posed a barrier to the corporate dream of total ideological hegemony. Clearly, the model for social control that was erected in the twenties was just that: *a model*. The general rises in the level of real wages were often outbalanced by the loss of areas of life which had traditionally been outside the arena of monetary exchange. Even though consumption became a way of life for increasing numbers, vast sectors of the population—black, brown, white, immigrant, native born—still lived within a world which had not yet been offered the opportunity to consume itself into social and political passivity. For these sectors, the expressed ideals of social betterment invited overt suppression more than they provided an opening for neutralization by consumption.

With the stock market crash and the Depression, the model for total consumerism was no answer to radical sentiments which had not been either "answered" or effectively eradicated by repression. Some drawing their tone from the old IWW, others from the populist and ethnic radicalisms of the recent past, some from the emerging spectre of world communism, still others from a consideration of their immediate circumstances, Americans in the thirties began to refer openly to socialism as a way out of the crisis of capitalism. While the advertising industry prospered, attempting to keep corporate names in the mind's eye of the populace, the corporate ideal generated within the New Deal tried to blend socialistic demands with a commitment to a highly organized preservation of the social order.[8] During the thirties, goods advertisers waited for a better selling day and reminded people that the products would be there when needed. Beyond the realm of goods, media were mobilized· to sell what *could* be bought: a spirit of fraternity and commitment, a sense of justice within a vigorously conserved sense of order. The popular arts and cinema enjoyed a heyday. The radio became an integral tool of politics and culture. These combined to generate an ideology of raw frontier idealism and moral commitment: an idealism of acceptable scarcity, resiliant cultural fiber, social realism, hard work and fortitude.

In the midst of this cultural mobilization, the state was expanding its functions in a way which would prove decisive for the future. It was becoming the organizational principle of industry. While unbridled industry had been an effective apparatus for the early accumulation of capital and an expanded productive machinery, the state was now entering a period of development in which it would act to absorb surplus capital through the institution of services (public works, social security, etc.) and by becoming itself a major consumer of labor and of "overproduced" goods. With the expanded production called for by World War II, the policy of government spending moved from one of being a stopgap measure to being a policy that would "strike oil" for American business. A wide sector of economic activity opened up—never to be demobilized following World War II—in the form of war ("defense") industries. The ideal of permanent industrial productivity seemed to find its realization in these industries of war. War, programmed obsolescence, stockpiling and the governmental policy of unbelievable expenditure for "defense" all contributed to the notion that *here* was a sector of industry which could flourish in spite of people's ability or proclivity to be mass consumers. Alongside of the consumer industries, government purchase (and lucrative export to "allies") of goods, particularly costly war devices, created an open field for industrial expansion and "health."

Coming out of the Second World War, state consumption and the financial seeding of foreign markets infused money not merely into corporate coffers, but also created apparently stable employment for wide sectors of a population whose lives had been chronically characterized by the instability and disquietude of deprivation. Government loans to G.I. families and others helped to erect suburban communities which would prove to be fertile soil for the cultivation of a consumer Eden.

The jolt of energy provided by the postwar boom was like a miraculous tonic for a commercial culture which had been under siege since its nineteenth-century industrialization. The fierce explosion within the economy—wrought in war—provided a context within which the ideological pacification, initiated in the twenties, might begin to take effect for a wider sector of American society than ever before.

It was in the 1950s that the proffered dreams of the captains of consciousness, worked out in the twenties, really began to take concrete form. It was a period of monumental change. The commodity market parodied the patterns of "conspicuous consumption" that Thorstein Veblen had noted among rich capitalists and middle-class imitators at the turn of the century, this time "democratized" on a mass scale. The mass marketing of television (invented in 1925) carried the consumer imagery into the back corners of home life. The vision of the *modern family* informed a suburban migration which dwarfed (five fold) even the massive European migration to these shores in the first decade of the century.[10] The shift of work and commercial activity into arenas of bureaucracy, service and communications further minimized the notion of popular self-sufficiency. The new society was one which distributed *culture* on a mass scale. This triumph over the locality of people's lives as a source of nurturement and information is, perhaps, the monumental achievement of twentieth-century capitalism: centralization of the social order.

Yet even if the postwar boom provided a topsoil for capitalist regeneration and expansion, the social crises of mass society continued—revealed in the social and political contours of life in the fifties and erupting again in the sixties and seventies.

The New Deal had, in many ways, continued the ideological project begun in the twenties. Within its vast social mobilization, and riddled throughout its projects for public works, the New Deal had made monumental use of artists, writers, other cultural workers, and pioneer efforts in radio broadcasting, within what was the most successful public relations program that had yet been seen. But within the reality of material scarcity, much of this public relations did not mesh well with the corporate image of mass consumerism and industrial beneficence. As the United States edged toward recovery, in the early days after entry into the Second World War, it was clear to businessmen that the corporate image had suffered dearly in the preceding decade or so. Speaking bluntly of the *content* of New Deal public relations, U.S. Chamber of Commerce president Eric Johnston noted its most obvious shortcoming. "The main evil of the New Deal period," he explained, "was its spirit of vendetta and class warfare."[11]

In the period following the war, the project of ideological consumerization—begun in the twenties—began to reemerge. Combining the social and technological developments of the twenties with the component of economic boom that characterized the fifties, the postwar era was one in which mass consumption erupted, for increasing numbers, into a full-blown style of life. In the suburbs that had sprung up with such marked rapidity, a social sphere had been forged that was removed from the urban-industrial center yet totally dependent upon it for its sustenance; the suburbs were a contained representation of open space—there was little reality within which yeoman self-sufficiency could grow. Television, an esoteric invention some twenty-five years prior, became the common synonym for mass communications: a futuristic analogue to the hearth. Situated in the midst of the American household, TV became a vehicle for a consumerist mentality. Before the fifties, electronic media had already made a momentous entry into Americans' lives, significantly altering the notion of "communication." With the fifties, however, this alteration reached mammoth proportions. Consumerist ideology became rampant, critical social thought became anathema. Beyond the specific messages of the media, a quantitative impact was manifested. Before the fifties, both radio and television had generally stopped broadcasting at ten o'clock in the evening. In 1950, with the first ventures into late-night television, this began to change. The notion that there should be time and space which were inappropriate for commercial penetration began to vanish. The total realm of existence had become "fair game;" the option of privacy was being challenged around the clock.

Consumption was inherent to the life style of the 1950s television situation comedy. The comic impetus was often drawn from a consumerized context—the *wife* going overboard on a $40 hat was one of the all-time favorite plot devices. While a consumption-defined *middle-class* existence was proffered in shows and bolstered by the flashy beginnings of modern television advertising, working-class life was chiefly characterized by the laughable boorishness of the family breadwinner. Two of the most *popular* shows of the fifties, William Bendix in *Life of Riley* and Jackie Gleason's *Honeymooners*, made much of the supposed idiocy of working-class life. In both these "working-class" comedies, were it not for the middle-class-minded wives—loyal consumers—the working men could hardly make it through the day. Over and over again, there was the spectacle of Ralph Kramden, the wind-bag busdriver played by Jackie Gleason, being "brought into line" by his wife, Alice, her arms forever burdened by the weight of omnipresent, recently purchased packages. In this and other such comedies, the normalcy of consumerism was defined and writ large in the living rooms of the American populace.

Quiz shows, common fare during the 1950s, projected an imagery of abundance and the easy accessibility of goods. On shows like the Goodson–Todman production of *The Price is Right*, the audience was not only treated to a parade of the wares of the marketplace but was vicariously rewarded for internalizing a blend of dependent infantilism and a correct sense of the actual retail prices ("WITHOUT GOING OVER!!!") of products. Indeed, the tag prices of all kinds of goods had become useful knowledge in a world in which these items were flooding market counters and being touted and screamed over by modern housewives on the TV giveaways.

While game shows and situation comedies provided a showcase for the new consumer-oriented America, television was also presenting a vision of the past which was laundered of conflict and divested of the horrors of industrial history. Western drama presented a common, pioneer heritage for industrial America, many of whose ancestors had borne little actual resemblance to heroic, law-abiding desperados like Hopalong Cassidy, Wyatt Earp or Davy Crockett. Immigrant life was either glorified, as in *I Remember Mama,* or denigrated as in the case of Molly Goldberg and her husband, Jake.

There was little room in these shows for the industrial hardship or social radicalism that had actually characterized the immigrant experience in America for many. *I Remember Mama* presented a version of immigrant life far removed from the sweatshops of the Lower East Side of New York or the steel mills of Homestead, Pennsylvania. Here was a robust Scandinavian family, well on its way to becoming solid Americans—and loving it. In its depiction of both the present and the past, television wrought a structure for past and present which would lead its audience to an uncompromising adulation for the market economy and the *universals* that it projected.

On television and on the consumer market, corporately produced goods and services were being reinforced as the cohesive fiber of daily life and as objects of fantasy. In the 1950s, automobiles took wings—literally and figuratively. The car became an all-out necessity for a suburbanized culture with a corporately engineered predisposition against mass transport. Cars also became the embodiment of escape fantasy. As the small plots of land that typified tract housing developments carried the connotation of "open spaces," the automobiles which carried people there were infused with a similar depiction of wish fulfillment. Autos, from the mid-fifties on, took on a swept-wing appearance; many had "cockpits" styled more to Buck Rogers' specifications than designed to be functional for driving on the road. The bigger the fins, the classier the car. Cadillac, Lincoln and Chrysler Imperial led in the space race. At the same time, automobiles provided getaway space for teenage sex—although this possibility had revealed itself much earlier. The advertised aura which was surrounding these cars was one of escape from the crowding of urban industrial life. The purchase of these cars, and the increasing reality of bumper-to-bumper traffic jams, however, only increased the congestion and pressure of daily existence.

In all of this, the vision of the *good life* which had been set forth on the pages of the *Ladies' Home Journal,* the *Saturday Evening Post,* and *True Story* magazine in the twenties was becoming pervasive, infused with the frantic and patriotic fervor of the fifties. The consumer-ized universe was being erected with unprecedented vigor, positing an economic nationalism which signified the inviolate sanctity of the world of goods. The defini-tions of "freedom" and "choice" were being unified and firmly implanted in the conception of loyal commitment to the political, religious and social arenas encrusted by brand names and consumer credit. Once again, the definition proffered by a "freedom-loving" political ideology was one in which to produce one's own world was subversive (except where it was legitimized by the "do-it-yourself" industry); to assert the idea that a community might control its own destiny was "communistic." While in certain cases the centralization of authority took on a progressive bent—as in the attack on state's rights which formed a legal wedge for the move to racial integration of schools—the general tenor of centralized power indicated the growing presence of corporate planning in the organization of daily life. Immigrant cultures, on the levels of social interaction and their traditional political activities, were *American-ized* by corporate imagery and replaced by a homoge-nous vision of what it meant to be a citizen. The common parlance of citizenship was characterized by a ready familiarity with the American "way of life," replete with television, new cars, lawn mowers and "fast" foods. Physical appearance was also a vehicle for committing oneself to Americanism. The marketplace was gorged with the uniforms of citizenship. For women, a blonde, milk-fed image of beauty and purity was posed against the "dark" feminity of less godly cultures and social orders. For some Jewish women, entering the middle class from the "unsavory" quarters of their past, peroxide and plastic surgeons attempted to wipe out all physical traces of racial deviation. For Jewish men, beards and long hair became increasingly anathema—signs of being either "beatniks" or worse yet, "dark-visaged" communists. Ethnic names were anglicized, spawning a score of Italian-American vocalists whose backgrounds were miraculously transplanted to Sherwood Forest.

For the nonwhite population, the cultural integration was less concerted. While white culture industries certainly drew from black music for ideas, the decidedly white imagination of advertising and corporate culture only reinforced the exclusionary and racist sensibility of the new culture. Perhaps this is part of the reason why the white cultural tranquility of the fifties was so disrupted by the black civil rights movement, the main domestic force of open political and social opposition during the period. If the commercial culture posed passive consumerism in white terms, those who were unable to participate in this giant barbecue (largely nonwhite people) were clearly left to their own devices. Only in the late 1960s, with the commercial culture under siege from many fronts, did the advertising industry begin to address a black audience, offering a vision of bland consumer culture in different shades.

Insofar as the advertised spectacle of the good life told Americans how to live, the political and social climate gave a firm indication of what would not be acceptable. To look *different*; to act *different*; to think *different*; these became the vague archetypes of subversion and godlessness. Alongside the messages of how Americans should live and what it meant to participate in the society of abundance, there were clear messages as to what constituted violations of these dicta. The virulent anticommunism of the 1950s was, on the surface, an attack on an immoral, highly centralized authoritarian apparatus that found its source in the Soviet Union. But it contained a wider perspective. Under its broad umbrella of conformity lay a general attack on any social perspective which contended that social change came from the people.

As the cold war worked its way under the skin of American life, it posed an idealized, consumerized, and increasingly advertised vision of *people* as basically inadequate. This was at its core. While anticommunist rhetoric never confronted the question directly, consumerized conformity was posed violently against a mode of thought which explored the possibility of people emerging as heroes of their own history. The vision of freedom which was being offered to Americans was one which continually relegated people to consumption, passivity and spectatorship. Those who questioned this chain of command were labeled "communist." Where the impulse toward self-determination took on an artistic or easily isolated form, it was categorically dismissed as "beatnik" or "avant-garde."

The conformism which seems to have emerged as the characteristic idiom of the fifties was (as in the case of the twenties) bolstered by the employment of political terror. Little children were given food for thought, continually being sent diving under their desks to avoid the imminence of a Soviet A-Bomb attack. These air-raid measures would have been little real help in avoiding the ravages of holocaust, but they did rein-force the well-schooled polarity between the American "way of life" and what John Foster Dulles repeatedly cited as "Godless Communism." The Red Scare was transported into every home via the televised McCarthy hearings. The execution of Ethel and Julius Rosenberg indicated that not only were communist leadership and "Pinko" Hollywood hotshots vulnerable, but that an everyday American family could be sought out and destroyed if it weren't careful. In the midst of this deplorable masquerade of omnipotence, many Ameri-cans went into cultural hiding, destroying or secreting all traces of differentiation. If differentiation was an indicator of disloyalty, then the monochromatic, stan-dardized integrants of a vigorously consumed existence could provide a safe persona during this difficult and, for many, terrifying period. More than a vehicle for the good life, self-definition by commodities pointed the way to a safe life.

In the years following World War II, the trend toward cultural mobilization reached epic proportion. Television was carrying corporate culture into what was to become a vast majority of American homes. The expansion of bureaucracies and of service industries was defining an increasing sector of the social processes according to a centralized corporate logic. More than pervasive, the injection of corporate bonding into the interstices of existence was altering and attempting to safely standardize the common perception of daily life. While heralding a world of unprecedented freedom and opportunity, corporations (in concert with the state apparatus) were generating a mode of existence which was increasingly regimented and authoritarian. If consumer culture was a parody of the popular desire for self-determination and meaningful community, its innards revealed the growing standardization of the social terrain and corporate domination over what was to be consumed and experienced.

While the decade of the fifties was largely one of containment, a time of social and political petrification, the explosive years that followed revitalized the domain of public opposition and militancy. Ironically, as the cultural apparatus attempted to compensate for the confinements of the productive society, it was in the realm of the culture that growing resistance focused most sharply. From different fronts within an increasingly corporatized society came indications that the cultural apparatus of consumerism provided a rich soil for discontent as well as complacency.

First, the social landscape was attacked and disrupted by those who were most ignored in its parameters. While during the Depression scarcity had conformed to a multiracial ideology, creating a kind of "We're all in this thing together" mentality, the culture of the fifties reiterated the notion of class along the lines of *who could* and *who could not* buy their way to *happiness*. Industry was moving South, agriculture was stagnating or being mechanized, and on both fronts it was the black population that was bearing the brunt of the transformation. The postwar movement among blacks—first in the South, then continuing and extending into the cities of the North—represented a beginning of resistance that came from that part of the population which was most noticeably being ignored on the level of gainful employment and by the social program of consumerization.

If black resistance was related to an exclusion from the corporate social network, other resistance was born of familiarity. It grew among those for whom the cultural web of consumerism was being most elaborately and intricately spun: the children and women of the *consumer culture*.[12] Where for their grandparents and parents it had been the productive apparatus, its fragmentary routines and standardization, which gave ground to discontent, the standardization of culture, flourishing after World War II, broadened alienation even more. As corporately determined patterns tempered the realm of daily existence, the degradation of labor gave way to a broad degradation of social life *per se*.[13] The commercialization of culture, attempting to reproduce corporate priorities in the wide social realm, tended also to broaden the scope of opposition.

Within the advertised life style, young people and their mothers had been the *social principles* of the consumer ethic. Men were expected to act out corporate commands primarily in job-defined ways. For women and children, the corporate ideal was geared toward a definition of home and community life. If "home" was a man's refuge from the work-a-day world, for mothers and children it was expected to be a place where their own form of commitment to that world was acted out. Daily life was expected to be carried out according to the conformities of consumption. Amidst a promise of unlimited possibilities, women and children confronted limited and predigested realities. Among the children and women whose lives were encased by the commercialized democracy, the competitiveness, obedience and confinement implied in the corporate version of social life took its most definite toll.

Within the student movement of the 1960s and the rebirth of feminism that followed lay the sense that the social realm, the realm in which life reproduces life, was becoming increasingly authoritarian and repressive. Integral to the politics of the New Left was a recognition that social space was severely circumscribed by a repressive corporate order. In the twenties, advertising and consumerism had stood as a corporate alternative to what had been a chronically oppressive industrial situation. For the youth culture of the sixties, advertising posed no such alternative. Raised within the all-pervasive aura of mass consumption, students in the "movement" confronted advertised culture as their common memory, their basic definition of corporate life itself. The New Left confronted the "quality of life" beyond the industrial factory, out in the broader social realms which corporate organization was set on conquering.

The reemergence of feminism in the late 1960s betrayed parallel developments. The tension between the imagery of "housewife" and the growing involvement of women in the job market had been irritating in the twenties. In the fifties and sixties this irritation had erupted into a festering wound. With more women than ever employed in clerical work and service activities (corporate housekeeping and nurturing roles), "wifely" personae that encouraged isolation and a sense of social irrelevancy persisted, even as the domestic realm was steadily being devaluated within the priorities of the broad, corporate society.

Women's politics, the critique of sexual objectification and of "male chauvinism," became focused on the home situation. The home was a seeming anachronism, being reproduced and reinforced by the unresponsive corporate vision. The "home," the "husband," became a shorthand for the social denigration of women within corporate society.

Within the robotized veneer of the fifties lay the heart of the resistance that was to emerge. Beginning with a perception of the "one-dimensionality" and "loneliness" of social existence, today the critique has come full circle, confronting the world of work. As evidenced by our recent history, the barbarity and boredom of working conditions has been dramatized in the widespread opposition to corporate regimentation. Strikes and job actions against speed-up and enforced overtime are united with a critique of consumerism; both working conditions and consumption stand inadequate to meet the expression of human needs.

From the late sixties on there has been a proliferation of cultural movements which have expanded the scope of opposition. As resistance has mounted, however, the captains of consciousness have hardly thrown in the towel. Appropriating the lingo and styles of the New Left, the counterculture, feminism, neoagrarianism, ethnicity, drug-vision and other phenomena, the advertising industry, seeking markets, has generated a mass culture which reflects the spirit but not the cutting edge of this resistance. While advertising of the twenties spoke against the deprivations of scarcity, an increasing amount of today's advertising and product imagery speak to the deprivations of what has been called "abundance." Within advertising, the social realm of resistance is reinterpreted, at times colonized, for corporate benefit. Ads mirror the widespread judgment that mass-produced goods are junky and unhealthy. Products are advertised as if they contain this anticor-

porate disposition—praised for their organic natural-
ness and their timeless quality. Modes of anticorporate
resistance and sentiment reappear in the ads themselves, miraculously encased within the universal terms
of the market. General Mills reinforces corporate hegemony in the name of natural cereals—a harkening to
a precorporate, idealized past. The automobile industry
offers machines for wish fulfillment—at the same time
hoping to contain those wishes within the domain of the
cash nexus. From the oil industry comes a more authoritarian image to confront the loci of resistance. Oil
industry ads are singular in their ability to say, "We
know you don't like things as they are, but we're the boss
and that's the way it is!" Most other ads tend, however,
to offer a way out of the corporate bummer. On both
the material and psychological levels, advertising offers
refuge from an overly managed and infiltrated social
space.

As we are confronted by the mass culture, we are
offered the idiom of our own criticism as well as its
negation—corporate solutions to corporate problems.
Until we confront the infiltration of the commodity
system into the interstices of our lives, *social change* itself
will be but a product of corporate propaganda. There
have been the beginnings of a politics of daily life. This
politics has already been subjected to the ironies of that
which it opposes. As the politics of domestic government is linked to the politics of daily life, there must be
an unrelenting vigilance against and rejection of the
corporation mode of amelioration.

The triumph of capitalism in the twentieth century
has been its ability to define and contend with the
conditions of the social realm. From the period of the
1920s, commercial culture has increasingly provided an
idiom within which desires for social change and fanta-

sies of liberation might be articulated and contained. The cultural displacement effected by consumerism has provided a mode of perception that has both confronted the question of human need and at the same time restricted its possibilities. Social change cannot come about in a context where objects are invested with human subjective capacities. It cannot come about where commodities contain the limits of social betterment. It requires that people never concede the issue of who shall define and control the social realm.

NOTES

PREFACE

1 Henry Adams, *The Education of Henry Adams* (1918), p. 380.
2 E. E. Cummings, untitled, *Complete Poems, 1913–1962* (1972), p. 248.
3 Sonny Terry and Brownie McGhee, "Your Motor ain't Runnin'," in concert, September 1973.
4 See E. P. Thompson, *The Making of the English Working Class* (1964). For anyone not familiar with this work, its insights and information into the social history of industrial capitalism are helpful for understanding the human experience of modern life.
5 Herbert G. Gutman, "Work, Culture, and Society in Industrializing America," *American Historical Review*, 78, No. 3 (June 1973), 531–588. Of all the recent work and thought on American labor history, Gutman's is among the most impressive. Linking demographic and literary sources, his use of both reflects a historical sensitivity not seen in most such work.
6 Karl Marx, "Preface to a Contribution to the Critique of Political Economy," *Marx-Engels Selected Works*, Vol. I (Moscow, 1962), 362–363.
7 E. P. Thompson, "Time, Work-Discipline, and Industrial Capitalism," *Past and Present*, 38 (December 1967), 56–97.
8 *Ibid.*, p. 97.

9 For some basic works depicting the labor struggles of the period see Jeremy Brecher, *Strike* (1972); Philip S. Foner, *History of the Labor Movement in the United States* (1947); Norman Ware, *The Industrial Worker, 1840–1860* (1924); Norman Ware, *The Labor Movement in the United States, 1860–1895* (1929).

10 Much evidence of this can be seen in the Massachusetts Bureau of Statistics of Labor, *Report*, particularly for the early 1870s. Edited by George MacNeill, a confidant and friend of the Eight-Hour Movement in New England, the *Reports* contain much revealing narrative material as well as certain political documents of the struggles.

11 Ira Steward, "Poverty," Massachusetts Bureau of Statistics of Labor, *Report* (1873), pp. 411–439. Steward was the leading ideologue of the New England Eight-Hour Movement and formulated a program of worker-run cooperatives which could, he felt, place working people in a position to increasingly define the mode of production by their collective consumption of goods. His discussion of poverty is quite interesting. Rather than defining it in terms of the quantity of goods or wages that a given family or individual would live on, Steward defined poverty in terms of the social relations between the individual and industry. Thus, to Steward, a clerical worker who might think of him/herself as "middle-classed" owing to slightly higher wages, lived under an ideological illusion. The extra wage in no way reflected a greater level of worker self-definition within the industrial context. The clerical worker's relationship to corporate power was hardly different from that of an industrial laborer. Rather, the extra wage earned by the "white-collar" worker (as we might define him today) was but a bonus with which the worker could buy certain goods to create the appearance of higher class status. It was no more than that. The difference in wage or apparent lifestyle was, to Steward, an illusory difference, but one that divided the lives and aspirations of working people whose true needs could be found only in unity.

I have discussed Steward's work, as well as the work of one of his disciples in "George Gunton: The Capitalization of the Cosmos," unpublished manuscript, 1969.

12 This view is represented in Robert K. Murray, *Red Scare: A Study of National Hysteria, 1919–1920* (1955).

13 Dale Yoder, *Labor Attitudes in Iowa and Contiguous Territory* (1929). This is a study of workers' feelings on business, under-

taken by the Iowa Bureau of Business Research. It is filled with many narrative first-hand accounts as well as samples from the local labor press, and should be of interest to students of twentieth-century labor history.

14 Editorial, *Union Advocate and Public Forum* (Sioux City, Iowa, March 30, 1928).

15 The American Federation of Labor (AFL) is perhaps the most obvious example of a union structure which had committed itself to the wage demand.

16 *Union Advocate and Public Forum* (Sioux City, March 30, 1928).

17 Yoder, p. 85.

18 Feature article, *Tri-City Labor Review* (Rock Island, Illinois, April 13, 1932).

19 Siegfried Giedion, *Mechanization Takes Command* (1948), p. 122.

20 Thomas Edison, *The Emancipator* (December 28, 1912), quoted in Allan Nevins, *Ford: The Times, The Man, The Company* (1954), p. 532.

21 See Loren Baritz, *Servants of Power; A History of the Use of Social Science in American Industry* (1960).

22 Meyer Bloomfield, "The New Profession of Handling Men," *Annals of the American Academy of Political and Social Science*, LXI (September 1915), p. 122.

23 *System, The Magazine of Business* (Chicago 1917), p. 3.

24 Gerd Korman, *Industrialization, Immigrants and Americanizers: The View From Milwaukee, 1866–1921* (1967), p. 91. Examples of the integration of "welfare" work and factory discipline may be seen in the materials developed for teaching English to immigrant workers at International Harvester's Weber plant in 1911. These selections from the lessons are found in Korman, pp. 144–145, and are drawn from *Harvester World*, 3:31 (March 1912):

> I hear the whistle. I must hurry.
>
> I hear the five minute whistle.
>
> It is time to go to the shop.
>
> I take my check for the gate board and hang it on the department board.
>
> I change my clothes and get ready to work.
>
> The starting whistle blows.
>
> I eat lunch.

It is forbidden to eat until then.

The whistle blows at five minutes of starting time.

I get ready to go to work.

25 Margaret F. Byington, *Homestead: The Households of a Mill Town* (1910), p. 31, 22.

26 *Ibid.*, p. 31.

27 *Ibid.*, pp. 48–49, 55.

28 *Ibid.*, p. 65.

29 *Ibid.*, p. 124.

30 *Ibid.*, p. 172.

31 Meyer Bloomfield, p. 125.

32 Herbert W. Hess, "History and Present Status of the 'Truth-in-Advertising' Movement as Carried on by the Vigilance Committee of the Associated Advertising Clubs of the World," *Annals of the American Academy of Political and Social Science*, CI (May 1922), p. 211.

PART I

1 Alfred Dupont Chandler, *Giant Enterprise, Ford, General Motors and the Automobile Industry* (1964), p. 29. Chandler is citing the *Federal Trade Commission Report on the Motor Vehicle Industry.*

2 *Ibid.*, p. 26.

3 ". . . during a period of eighteen years commencing in 1908, Ford Motor Company manufactured and offered for sale only one basic model of passenger automobile. . . . This was the [black] Model T." See Chandler, pp. 27, 37.

4 Harold Loeb, *National Survey of Potential Product Capacity* (1935), p. 3.

5 This may be seen as a response to a combination of things. Aside from the fact of proliferating mass production methods, the 1921 depression/buyers' strike served as an impetus to this study.

6 Edward A. Filene, *The Way Out: A Forecast of Coming Changes in American Business and Industry* (1924), p. 93.

7 Chandler, p. 143.

8 Notably Alfred P. Sloan of General Motors. Sloan saw productive strategy in broad social terms. His biography, *My Life With General Motors* (1960), gives an account of these early developments.

9 Loeb, p. xv, in regard to "the capacity of the nation to produce

goods and services. If full advantage were taken of existing resources, man power, and knowledge . . . every new invention, every improved method, every advance in management technique will increase the final quantitative estimate." Such a question would be answered by "a running inventory of our approach to perfection rather than a research into existing capacity as determined by production." The survey considered such a potential too open-ended to effect meaningful speculation.

10 Edward A. Filene, *The Consumer's Dollar* (1934), p. 13.

11 Editorial, "The Phantom of National Distribution," *Printers' Ink* (hereafter, *P.I.*), CXXIV, No. 12 (September 20, 1923), p. 180. As the trade journal for the ad industry dating back into the nineteenth century, *Printers' Ink* is an invaluable source for any research in this field.

12 Ernest Elmo Calkins, *Business the Civilizer* (1928), p. 10

13 Filene, *The Consumer's Dollar*, p. 29.

14 Filene, *The Way Out*, p. 50.

15 Loren Baritz, *The Servants of Power* (1960), p. 15.

16 Whiting Williams, *Mainsprings of Men* (1925), p. 297.

17 Whiting Williams, *What's on the Worker's Mind* (1920), p. 317.

18 Filene, *The Way Out*, pp. 62–63.

19 Williams, *Mainsprings*, p. 51.

20 Filene, *The Way Out*, p. 127.

21 *Ibid.*, p. 137.

22 Williams, *Mainsprings*, p. 127.

23 By the 1920s widespread elements of the union movement had accepted such an ideology. Among others, William English Walling of the Labor Progressives dissolved the class struggle in one fell swoop. Virtually paraphrasing the ideologues of scientifically planned capitalism, he felt that "to bring labor to the maximum productivity, the American labor movement believes, requires new organization and policies in the administration of industry." See William Walling, *American Labor and American Democracy* (1926), p. 233.

Walling spoke of *labor* and *consumer* as interrelated aspects of the total life of the American worker. His concern for consumer rights reflected the ideology of progressive capital no less than did the writings of Edward Filene, who, although he had one foot in the "consumer category," placed his other on the side of financial power rather than in the monotony of factory life.

24 Norman Ware, *Labor in Modern Industrial Society* (1935), p. 88.
25 Walling, p. 212.
26 *Ibid.*
27 In an attempt to assure that his workers carried on a "moderate" life off of the job, Ford developed a *Sociological Department* staffed by thirty investigators who were "empowered to go into the workers' homes to make sure that no one was drinking too much, that everyone's sex life was without blemish, that leisure time was profitably spent, that no boarders were taken in, that houses were clean and neat." Baritz, p. 33.
28 Ware, *Labor in Modern Industrial Society*, p. 101.
29 *Ibid.*, p. 94.
30 Williams, *What's on the Workers' Mind*, p. 299.
31 Filene, *The Way Out*, p. 202.
32 Ware, *Labor in Modern Industrial Society*, p. 95. According to Ware's studies, union manufacturing labor averaged 40–48 hours per week. Nonunion labor in similar industries averaged 50 hours per week, while labor in more traditional areas, mills and shops, worked 48–60 hours per week.
33 *Ibid.*, pp. 16–17.
34 Robert S. Lynd, "The People as Consumers," *Recent Social Trends in the United States: Report of the President's Research Committee on Social Trends*, Vol. II (1933), p. 862. Such credit buying was initiated primarily in the automobile industry with the General Motors Acceptance Corporation (GMAC).
35 Walter Dill Scott, *Influencing Men in Business* (originally published 1911; 1928 revised edition enlarged by Delton T. Howard), p. 133, 1928 edition.
36 Williams, *What's on the Worker's Mind*, p. 317.
37 "In some lines, such as whiskey and milk, distribution cost is from four to ten times the cost of production." Chandler, p. 157.
38 Harry Tipper, et al., *Advertising: Its Principles and Practice* (1921), pp. 16–18. See also, Alvin Bunisicker, "Stabilizing Profits Through Advertising," *P.I.*, CXXIV, No. 13, p. 81.
39 Frank Spencer Presbrey, *The History and Development of Advertising* (1929), p. 620.
40 Calkins, p. 236.
41 Presbrey, p. 625.
42 Editorial, "Senator Borah on Marketing," *P.I.*, CXXIV, No. 5 (August 2, 1923), p. 152.
43 Editorial, "The Phantom of National Distribution," *P.I.*, CXXIV, No. 12 (September 20, 1923), p. 180.

44 Baritz, p. 27.
45 *Ibid.*, p. 26.
46 Williams, *Mainsprings.*
47 Floyd Henry Allport, *Social Psychology* (1924), p. 325.
48 Calkins, p. 123.
49 Scott, p. 3.
50 Baritz, p. 26.
51 Scott, p. 132.
52 Baritz, p. 26.
53 Carl A. Naether, *Advertising to Women* (1928), p. 97.
54 "When we stop to consider the part which advertising plays in the modern life of production and trade, we see that basically it is that of education . . . it makes new thoughts, new desires and new actions." Presbrey, p. 620.
55 Scott, p. 43.
56 "Physical or sex attraction . . . other things being equal, qualities which make one pleasing to look at or to caress render their possessor popular to many and loved by not a few." Allport, p. 365.
57 Not incidental to this direct appeal to the consumer's self-image, advertisers argued that "heavy expenditures for consumer advertising by a manufacturer . . . [might] induce merchants to favor him with orders." Harold Maynard, et al., *Principles of Marketing* (1927), p. 439.
58 Presbrey, p. 622.
59 Robert S. Lynd and Helen Merrill Lynd, *Middletown* (1929), p. 82.
60 *Ibid.*, pp. 81–82.
61 Frederick Parker Anderson, "'Conscious' Advertising Copy," *P.I.*, CXXXVI, No. 8 (August 19, 1926), p. 130.
62 In "The People as Consumers," Robert Lynd further characterized the advertising of products of mass technology in terms of the questions of "uniformity" and the nature of the modern capitalist marketplace.

"Technological uniformity and complexity . . . tends to remove further the complex of characteristics blanketed by a brand name from the sorts of empirical comparisons that were more often possible a generation ago. . . . There is a ceaseless quest for what advertising men call 'million dollar ideas' . . . to disguise commodities still further by identifying them with cryptic characteristics." *Recent Social Trends*, I, pp. 876–877.
63 Roy Dickinson, "Freshen Up Your Product," *P.I.*, CL, No. 6 (February 6, 1930), p. 163.
64 Presbrey, p. 613.

65 *Ibid.*, p. 622.
66 *Ibid.*, p. 608.
67 *Ibid.*, p. 610.
68 George I. Krem, "The Foreign Language Market Wants Facts With Proof," *P.I.*, CXL, No. 5 (August 4, 1927), p. 108.
69 See Presbrey, "Illustrated Appendix."
70 *Ladies' Home Journal* (May 1924), p. 161.
71 *Ibid.*, p. 133.
72 Carl Albert Naether noted that "Woman buys 80–90% of all things in general use in daily life." The breakdown of this generalization specified: 96% of the dry goods, 87% of the raw and market foods, 67% of the automobiles, 48% of the drugs, etc. Naether, p. 4 (citing figures from Hollingsworth, *Advertising and Selling*). •

PART II

1 Edward A. Filene, *Successful Living in the Machine Age* (1931), p. 12.
2 *Forbes' Magazine* (April 1927).
3 John Adams, quoted by Herbert Gutman, "Work, Culture, and Society in Industrializing America, 1815–1919," *American Historical Review*, 78, No. 3 (June 1973), p. 532.
4 In Gutman's article (above) there is the best extensive discussion of the recurrent tensions between indigenous working-class cultures (largely immigrant) and the problem of industrial organization and ideology. While Gutman's work tends to distill out working-class culture as autonomous and to view capitalism as an obstacle or impediment, rather than as a social system in which workers are involved, this in no way invalidates the value of his work.
5 Paul H. Nystrom, *Economic Principles of Consumption* (1929), p. 5.
6 Jacques Ellul, *Technological Society* (1967).
7 *Printers' Ink: A Journal for Advertisers, Fifty Years: 1888–1938* (Special Edition), p. 397.
8 Pitkin is here quoted in James Rorty, *Our Master's Voice: Advertising* (1934), p. 392.
9 Edward L. Bernays, *Biography of an Idea: Memoirs of a Public Relations Counsel* (1965), p. 439.
10 Filene, *Successful Living*, p. 271.
11 *Ibid.*, p. 272, 144.
12 *Ibid.*, pp. 145–146.

13 *Ibid.*, p. 157.
14 Robert S. Lynd and Helen Merrill Lynd, *Middletown* (1929), p. 22.
15 Filene, *Successful Living*, p. 14.
16 Leverett S. Lyon, "Advertising," *The Encyclopedia of the Social Sciences*, Vol. I, (1922), p. 475.
17 In business writings and pronouncements on the problem of overproduction, the link is often drawn between this and the political/economic function of consumption.
18 Irving Bernstein, *The Lean Years* (1960), p. 54.
19 *Ibid.*, p. 61.
20 Robert S. and Helen Merrill Lynd, *Middletown*, pp. 254–256.
21 Max Horkheimer, "The End of Reason," *Studies in Philosophy and Social Science*, 9 (1941), p. 379.
22 *Ibid.*, p. 384.
23 Walter Dill Scott, *Increasing Human Efficiency in Business* (1917), p. 197.
24 The N. W. Ayer *Guide to Periodical Literature* lists the decline as follows:

    1900—2,120
    1920—2,042
    1930—1,942
The figures since 1930 bear out this trend:
    1940—1,878
    1950—1,772
    1956—1,760
25 Roy B. Nixon, "Concentration and Absenteeism in Daily Newspaper Ownership," *Journalism Quarterly* (June 22, 1945. Updated in 1954).

    Here, too, the post-1930 figures maintain the trend toward concentration and monopolization of the press:
    1940—87.3%
    1944/5—91.6%
    1953/4—94%
26 Robert E. Park, *The Immigrant Press and Its Control* (1922), p. 381.
27 *Ibid.*, p. 277.
28 *Report and Hearings of the Subcommittee on the Judiciary*, 66th Congress, Senate Document No. 62, "Brewing and Liquor Interests and German and Bolshevik Propaganda," U.S. Senate, Vol. I, pp. 465–472.
29 Park, p. 388.

30 Frances A. Kellor, *Immigrants in America: Program for a Domestic Policy*, (c. 1915), p. 8.
31 Frances A. Kellor, *Immigration and the Future* (1920), p. 101.
32 *Ibid.*, p. 102.
33 Park, p. 448.
34 *Ibid.*
35 *P.I.*, (June 5, 1914).
36 *Report and Hearings* (as above, note 28).
37 Park, p. 277.
38 Rorty, pp. 8–9.
39 Sherwood Anderson, *Letters* (1953), p. 135.
40 Rorty, p. 67.
41 James Agee, *Let Us Now Praise Famous Men*, 2nd ed. (1966), p. 13.
42 Bernays, *Biography of an Idea*, p. 439.
43 Refer to notes 12, 13, 14.
44 C. G. Jung, *The Undiscovered Self* (1958).
45 Horkheimer, "End of Reason," p. 379.
46 Georg Lukács, *History and Class Consciousness* (1971), p. 85.
47 Nystrom, *Economic Principles*, p. 78.
48 *P.I.*, LXXXVII (November 16, 1911), p. 17, 22.
49 D. A. Pope, "The Development of National Advertising, 1865–1920," (unpublished doctoral dissertation, Columbia University 1973), pp. 337–393.
50 Gilbert Russell, *Nuntius: Advertising and Its Future* (1926), p. 61.
51 Rorty, p. 176.
52 *Ibid.*, pp. 181–182.
53 George Harrison Phelps, *Tomorrow's Advertisers and their Advertising Agencies* (1929), p. 39.
54 *Printers' Ink Monthly*, 3 (February 1921), p. 31.
55 Phelps, p. 251
56 Russell, p. 77.
57 Phelps, pp. 4–5.
58 Gutman, p. 584.
59 Richmond, Virginia, *Whig*, June 15, 1886.
60 Edward A. Filene, "Mass Production Makes a Better World," *Atlantic Monthly* (May 1929), pp. 4–5, 8.
61 Paul H. Nystrom, *Economics of Fashion* (1928), p. 103.
62 Mark O'Dea, *A Preface to Advertising* (1937), p. 112.
63 *Printers' Ink: A Journal for Advertisers. Fifty Years: 1888–1938.* (1938), p. 362.
64 Helen Woodward, *Through Many Windows* (1926), p. 298. The question of how advertising, a product of industrial America,

could separate itself from the industrial context is an interesting one; it speaks to the process of communications of which national advertising was a prime area. While the ad industry was bureaucratically linked to the industrial machinery, its products were *capitalistic art forms* which publicly ignored complicity with much of the business world. The advertising industry's ability to perform such an obfuscation was deliberate. It was also located within the historical development of *media* to which advertising was related. Walter Benjamin, in "The Work of Art in the Age of Mechanical Reproduction" (1936), (*Illuminations*, 1968) has noted that as technologically reproduced art is designed for prolific exhibition, the notion of authenticity—the sense of there being an original—is lost. The essential element in each work of art is its immediacy, its every showing, rather than its ability to be located absolutely "in time and space." The consumer, confronted with a commercial advertisement, views but an offprint, not the economic-cultural apparatus from which it is generated, nor from his own life in relation to that apparatus. As such, he/she had only his/her critical abilities with which to draw the connections between "art" and its source. As the social style of technological corporatism, and art forms themselves, continually aim at manipulating those abilities to criticize— attempting, as Herbert Marcuse would have it, to *absorb all opposition*—that critical ability itself may tend to be domesticated. The *connection* between such art and its source may at times be reduced to a pacified epigram of modern life. It was, perhaps, the sense of immediacy that Benjamin described which may give advertising its particular value as an efficient tool of social productivity.

65 John B. Watson, "Psychological Care of Infant and Child," in Martin J. Sklar, *The Plastic Age* (1970), p. 315.
66 *Ibid.*, p. 309, 311.
67 Paul Mazur, quoted in the *New York Times* (November 29, 1931).
68 Phelps, pp. 151–152.
69 Kenneth M. Goode and Harford Powel, Jr., *What About Advertising* (1927), p. i.
70 Edward L. Bernays, *Propaganda* (1928), pp. 47–48.
71 Goode and Powel, pp. 102–103.
72 Phelps, p. 70.
73 *Ibid.*, p. 17.
74 *Ibid.*, p. 150.
75 Nystrom, *Economics of Fashion*, pp. 67–68.

76 Woodward, p. 345.
77 Robert S. and Helen Merrill Lynd, *Middletown*, p. 265.
78 Denys Thompson, *Voice of Civilisation: An Enquiry into Advertising* (1943), p. 109.
79 Filene, "Mass Production," p. 9.
80 Filene, *Successful Living*, p. 107.
81 *Ibid.*, p. 1.
82 Kellor, in *Advertising and Selling* (July 5, 1919), p. 2.
83 Nystrom, *Economic Principles*, p. 469.
84 Filene, *Successful Living*, p. 147.
85 Elizabeth Ellis Hoyt, *The Consumption of Wealth* (1928), p. v.
86 Horkheimer, "The End of Reason," p. 371.
87 Nystrom, *Economic Principles*, pp. 48–49.
88 Rorty, p. 145.
89 Nystrom, *Fashion*, p. 25.
90 Filene, *Successful Living*, p. 97.
91 *Ibid.*, p. 106.
92 *Ibid.*, p. 98.
93 *Ibid.*, p. 106.
94 Bernays, *Propaganda*, p. 31.
95 *Ibid.*
96 *Ibid.*, p. 21.
97 *Ibid.*, p. 9.
98 Nystrom, *Economic Principles*, p. 268.
99 Nystrom, *Fashion*, p. 26.
100 *Ibid.*, p. 9.
101 Hoyt, p. 95.
102 Rorty, p. 97.
103 Phelps, p. 251.
104 The idea that consumer protection was too large an issue to be dealt with on the level of consumers themselves pervades much of the literature of business. Arguing that consumer clubs require too much activity, too much work, and are not in accordance with the spirit of the new leisure, home economist Christine Frederick told women that they *should not* join consumer clubs. Rather, she argued, they should rely on existing channels: buying was a way of *voting* for good products, and federal and private (magazine and newspaper consumer testing departments) agencies should be relied upon as a source of judgment. See Christine Frederick, *Selling Mrs. Consumer* (1929), pp. 319–320.

Frederick went on to express the inadequate vantage point of the individual person as a consumer judge. Unschooled in the scientific expertise of industry, the consumer was deemed foolish to question the suggestions of advertising:

. . . criticizing Advertisements is one of the most illogical and dangerous past-times one might engage in, since the reader is never in a position to know all the sound reasons for a particular ad. [*Selling Mrs. Consumer*, p. 345]

Ad man Roy Durstine added that consumers, women in particular, should "base their information" on ads in acquiring sound goods for the home environment. Durstine denounced independent consumer evaluation groups as "autocratic," bent on the "control" of "human initiative." Roy S. Durstine, *This Advertising Business* (1929), pp. 38–39.

105 Stuart Chase and F. J. Schlink, *Your Money's Worth* (1927), p. 21.
106 Woodward, p. 204.
107 George Burton Hotchkiss, *Advertising Copy* (1924), p. 144.
108 O'Dea, pp. 7–9.
109 *Ibid.*, p. 94.
110 *Ibid.*, pp. 91–92.
111 *Ibid.*, p. 93.
112 Woodward, p. 220.
113 Claude C. Hopkins, *Scientific Advertising* (1923), p. 87.
114 *Ibid.*, p. 88.
115 Denys Thompson, p. 92.
116 *Ladies' Home Journal* (February 1928).
117 Frank Presbrey, *The History and Development of Advertising* (1929), "Advertising Appendix."
118 *Ibid.*
119 *Ibid.*
120 Phelps, p. 211.
121 Roland Barthes, *Mythologies* (1972), pp. 88–89.
122 Samuel Haber, *Efficiency and Uplift*, quoted in Kathy Stone, "The Origins of Job Structure in the Steel Industry," *Radical America*, 7, No. 6 (November-December 1973). Stone's article gives a good picture of the ideological and political function of technological development in industry.
123 Albert T. Poffenberger, "The Conditions of Belief in Advertising," *Journal of Applied Psychology*, VII, No. 1 (March 1923), pp. 1–9.

124 Siegfried Giedion, *Mechanization Takes Command* (1948), p. 609.
125 *Ibid.*, p. 607.

PART III

1 Lawrence K. Frank, "Social Change and the Family," *Annals of the American Academy of Political and Social Science*, CLX, (March 1932), p. 98.
2 The productive function and interaction of the precapitalist family is given an effective historical dimension in Philippe Ariès, *Centuries of Childhood* (1962). See also Alice Clark, *The Working Lives of Women in the Seventeenth Century* (1968) for a discussion of seventeenth-century home production as a mode of survival. Despite the English context of this work, her detailed study goes well into the question of artisanship of women and men and the ways in which industrial capitalism cut into the productive "partnership" of family life.

For a discussion of the nature of transformation between the pre-industrial family and that of the nineteenth century, see John Demos, "The American Family in Past Time," in *The American Scholar*, 43, No. 3 (Summer 1974), pp. 442–446.
3 Frank, p. 95.
4 Robert S. Lynd, "Family Members as Consumers," *Annals of the American Academy of Political and Social Science*, CLX, (March 1932), p. 87.
5 Robert S. Lynd, "The People as Consumers," *Recent Social Trends: Report of the President's Research Committee on Social Trends* (1933), pp. 902–906.
6 Gwendolyn Salisbury Hughes, *Mothers in Industry: Wage-Earning by Mothers in Philadelphia* (1925), p. 13.
7 The problem of whether or not women themselves related to their factory role was central to the Women's Trade Union League. The feeling of the League was that although women were increasingly working in factories, their identification with the home presented problems to their organization within unions. The following resolution, passed by the League in 1921, indicates that women's recurrent *home* role had to be especially attended to. The Women's Trade Union League, the resolution argued, must organize under the "recognition of the fact that many women do not remain permanently in industry and therefore that no opportunity should be lost to awaken their social consciousness for the sake of future moral support of the

labor movement." Gladys Boone, *The Women's Trade Union Leagues in Great Britain and the United States of America* (1942), p. 130.

8 Ernest Groves, *The American Family* (1934), p. 139.

9 Ernest Groves and William Fielding Ogburn, *American Marriage and Family Relationships* (1928), p. 346.

10 *Ibid.*, p. 349.

11 *Ibid.*, p. 353.

12 Chase Goring Woodhouse, "Money and Family Success," in Ernest Groves and Lee M. Brooks, *Readings in the Family* (1934), p. 185.

13 Groves and Ogburn, *American Marriage*, p. 24.

14 Frank, pp. 95–96.

15 Lynd, "Family Members as Consumers," p. 89.

16 Frank, pp. 95–96.

17 Viva Boothe, "Gainfully Employed Women in the Family," *Annals of the American Academy of Political and Social Science*, CLX (March 1932), p. 77.

18 *Ibid.*

19 Hughes, p. 33.

20 Boone, p. 130.

21 Hughes, p. 22.

22 *Ibid.*

23 Frank, p. 100.

24 Mrs. A. J. Graves, *Women in America* (1841), p. 164.

25 See Barbara Welter, "The Cult of True Womanhood: 1820–1860," *American Quarterly*, XVIII (Summer 1966), p. 162.

26 See Thorstein Veblen, *The Engineers and the Price System*. This conviction that the financial elites had become economically and socially outmoded is a dominant theme in Veblen's work and may be seen in a less systematic and developed argument in *Theory of the Leisure Class, Theory of Business Enterprise*, and *Absentee Ownership*. The last of these seems to have had the greatest influence on technocratic thought of the 1920s.

27 Charlotte Perkins Gilman Stetson, *Women and Economics* (1900), pp. 117–118.

28 *Ibid.*, p. 119, 145.

29 Floyd Dell, *Love in The Machine Age, A Psychological Study of the Transition from Patriarchal Society* (1930), p. 6.

30 *Ibid.*, p. 7.

31 Edward A. Filene, *Successful Living in the Machine Age* (1931), p. 96.

32 Gilman Ostrander, *American Civilization in the First Machine Age: A Cultural History of America's First Age of Technological Revolution and "Rule by the Young"* (1972), p.224

33 Filene, *Successful Living*, pp. 79–80.

34 Max Horkheimer, "Authoritarianism and the Family," in Ruth Wanda Aushen (ed.), *The Family: Its Function and Destiny* (1940), p. 383.

35 Antonio Gramsci, "Americanism and Fordism," *Prison Notebooks* (1971), pp. 296–297.

36 Christine Frederick, *Selling Mrs. Consumer* (1929), pp. 391–392.

37 William F. Ogburn, "The Family and Its Functions," *Recent Social Trends* (1933), p. 667.

38 Frederick, pp. 391–392.

39 Lynd, "Family Members as Consumers," p. 86.

40 *Ibid.*, p. 87.

41 Robert S. Lynd and Helen Merrill Lynd, *Middletown* (1929), p. 258, 134.

42 *Ibid.*, pp. 241–242.

43 The legal attack on child labor was spread out over the century, culminating in 1938 with the passage of the Fair Labor Standards Act. As child labor was most characteristic of agricultural production, the length of time it took for restrictions on child labor to develop must be correlated as an index of the industrialization of the culture.

The Fair Labor Standards Act stated that no child under 14 may work outside of school hours in non-manufacturing; under 16, no child may work during school hours; and under 18 may not work in occupations deemed hazardous by the Secretary of Labor. This is the current federal legal standard on child labor.

In the early part of this century half of the states placed restrictions on child labor, although such laws were enforced according to the demand for a labor force.

Organizations involved in the push for childlabor legislation included the National Consumer League (founded 1899) which was comprised of middle-class reformers and the National Child Labor Committee (founded 1904).

On the federal level, the establishment of the Children's Bureau in 1912 was followed in 1916 with the establishment of the Keating-Owen Act which forbade from interstate commerce articles produced by children. This legislation fared poorly and was repeatedly was struck down, given the still-widespread

demand for children workers in premechanized agricultural production. Only in 1938 with the Supreme Court support of the Fair Labor Standards Act did child labor legislation have security as an enforceable national policy.
See Grace Abbott, *The Child and the State* (1938); Robert H. Bremner, *From the Depths* (1956).

44 Robert S. and Helen Merrill Lynd, *Middletown*, p. 73.
45 Siegfried Giedion, *Mechanization Takes Command* (1948), p. 41.
46 Robert S. and Helen Merrill Lynd, *Middletown*, p. 73.
47 Irving Bernstein, *The Lean Years* (1960), p. 57.
48 Robert S. and Helen Merrill Lynd, *Middletown*, pp. 34–35.
49 *Ibid.*, p. 30.
50 Dell, p. 300.
51 Robert S. and Helen Merrill Lynd, *Middletown*, p. 30; see also Ruth Lindquist, *The Family in the Present Social Order* (1931), p. 83 for discussion of forced retirement practices.
52 Statistical materials correlating the population and work force composition give substance to such a contention. In terms of the work force itself, in 1890 the percentage of employed over-65 (men and women) was over 4.3% of the total. By 1930 the percentage had dropped below 4.1%.

Such figures are more dramatic when viewed in the context of the overall population. The numerical increase in people over 65 as compared to the numerical increase in those considered to be in the work force makes the question of the aged in production more startling. In the period between 1890 and 1930 the population of those over 65 tripled while the number of those in this age category who remained in the work force only doubled.

See Department of Commerce, *Historical Statistics of the United States, Colonial Times to 1957* (1960), p. 10 (Table A71–85), p. 71 (Table D–13–25), for figures on population and labor force, respectively.
53 Horkheimer, "The End of Reason," p. 381.
54 John B. Watson, *Behaviorism* (1924), p. 304.
55 Albert T. Poffenberger, *Psychology in Advertising* (1925), p. 35.
56 *Saturday Evening Post* (hereafter *SEP*), December 21, 1929.
57 *SEP*, December 7, 1929.
58 Robert S. and Helen Merrill Lynd, *Middletown*, p. 31.
59 Abraham Myerson, M.D., *The Nervous Housewife* (1929), pp. 113–114.
60 Ostrander's entire book argues this thesis.

61 *Ladies' Home Journal* (hereafter *LHJ*), January 1922.
62 Helen Woodward, *Through Many Windows* (1926), p. 314.
63 *LHJ*, June 1922.
64 *LHJ*, January 1922.
65 Lynd, "People as Consumers," p. 895.
66 *LHJ*, January 1922.
67 *Ibid.*
68 *LHJ*, July 1928.
69 "Mrs. Consumer of today [1929] is the sophisticated flapper of yesterday." Frederick, *Selling Mrs. Consumer*, p. 5.
70 See Carl B. Naether, *Advertising to Women* (1928); also Albert T. Poffenberger, *Psychology in Advertising* (1925), p. 592.
71 Filene, *Successful Living*, p. 96.
72 Quoted in Ostrander, p. 54.
73 Frank, p. 98.
74 Frederick, *Selling Mrs. Consumer*, p. 16, 14.
75 This ad is from an historical compendium of advertisements, Edgar R. Jones (ed.), *Those Were the Good Old Days: A Happy Look at American Advertising, 1880-1930* (1959). This volume is unpaginated. Listings are according to the year in which the ad appeared.
76 Frank S. Presbrey, *History and Development of Advertising* (1929) "Advertising Appendix."
77 *SEP*, December 7, 1929.
78 Jones (1924, 1925).
79 Jones (1928).
80 *SEP*, December 7, 1929.
81 Hughes, pp. 2-3.
82 Olive Schreiner, *Women and Labour* (1911), p. 68.
83 Edward Bernays, *Biography of an Idea*: Memoirs of a Public Relations Counsel (1965), pp. 386-387.
84 *SEP*, December 14, 1929.
85 *SEP*, December 7, 1929.
86 G. A. Nichols, "When Your Customers are Competitors," *Printers' Ink*, CXI (May 13, 1920), p. 52.
87 *LHJ*, May 1922.
88 Frederick, p. 169.
89 Lindquist, p. 43, 49.
90 Robert S. and Helen Merrill Lynd, *Middletown*, p. 133.
91 Frederick, p. 181.
92 Groves and Ogburn, p. 58.

93 Anna E. Richardson, "The Woman Administrator in the Mod ern Home," *Annals of the American Academy of Political and Social Science*, CLXIII (May 1929), p. 26.
94 Giedion, pp. 512ff.
95 Lillian Gilbreth, "Efficiency Methods Applied to Kitchen Design," *Architectural Record* (March 1930), p. 291.
96 Giedion, p. 517.
97 Meyerson, p. 260.
98 Presbrey, p. 592 and Frederick, pp. 12–13.
99 Lindquist, p. 14.
100 Benjamin R. Andrews, "The Home Woman as Buyer and Controller of Consumption," *Annals of the American Academy of Political and Social Science*, CLXIII (May 1929), p. 42.
101 *SEP*, December 7, 1929.
102 *SEP*, December 7, 1929.
103 *LHJ*, January 1926, July 1925.
104 D. B. Lucas and C. E. Benson, "The Historical Trend of Negative Appeals in Advertising," *Journal of Applied Psychology*, XIII, No. 4 (August 1929), p. 354.
105 Jones, (Lysol, 1926).
106 Hughes, pp. 18–19.
107 Andrews, p. 41.
108 Frederick, p. 15.
109 *Ibid.*, p. 5; pp. 129–130.
110 *Ibid.*, pp. 275–285.
111 Giedion, p. 616.
112 Frederick, p. 278.
113 *LHJ*, January 1922.
114 Robert S. and Helen Merrill Lynd, *Middletown*, pp. 267–268.
115 Lindquist, p. 73.
116 *LHJ*, July 1925.
117 *LHJ*, November 1928.
118 Robert S. and Helen Merrill Lynd, *Middletown*, p. 169.
119 *LHJ*, October 1928.
120 *LHJ*, October 1925.
121 In an informal survey of *LHJ* and *SEP* ads through the 1920s, I have found that between eight and ten ads per issue depict a woman at or looking into a mirror. Many of these ads are *not* for cosmetic products.
122 *LHJ*, March 1926.
123 Groves and Ogburn, p. 51.

124 *LHJ*, January 1922.
125 *LHJ*, May 1922.
126 *LHJ*, January 1922.
127 Naether, p. 252.
128 *Ibid.*, p. 248.
129 *Ibid.*, p. 129.
130 Naether, p. 100.
131 Mary E. Hoffman, *The Buying Habits of Small-Town Women* (1926), p. 11.
132 *LHJ*, July 1928.
133 Denys Thompson, p. 132. This copy is from a perfume advertisement.

CONSUMER REPORT

1 Vance Packard, *The Hidden Persuaders* (1957), p. 9.
2 Arnold Hauser, *The Social History of Art*, Vol. II (1952), p. 927.
3 Some writings which involve this intellectual trend include: Georg Lukàcs, *History and Class Consciousness* (1971); Herbert Marcuse, *One-Dimensional Man* (1964); Theodor Adorno, *Prisms* (1967); Harry Braverman, *Labor and Monopoly Capital* (1974); Martin J. Sklar, "On the Proletarian Revolution and the End of Political Economic Society," *Radical America*, Vol. III, No. 3 (May-June, 1969), pp. 1–41; Max Horkheimer, *The Eclipse of Reason* (1947), and also Horkheimer's *Critical Theory* (1972); Stanley Aronowitz, *False Promises* (1973).
4 This quote comes from a leader of the Molders' Union (1916), cited in Mike Davis, "The Stop Watch and the Wooden Shoe: Scientific Management and the Industrial Workers of the World," *Radical America*, Vol. VIII, No. 6 (January-February, 1975).
5 *Ibid.*, pp. 86–87.
6 Robert Franklin Hoxie, *Scientific Management and Labor* (1921), pp. 169–177.
7 Edgar Jones, *Those Were the Good Old Days* (1959), p. 439.
8 See Warren I. Susman, "The Thirties," in Stanley Cobden and Lorman Ratner (eds.), *The Development of an American Culture* (1970). This is the best discussion of political and social ideology during the decade of depression in the United States.
9 See Broadus Mitchell, *Depression Decade* (1947), for a discussion of the significance of World War II in the elevation of the United States out of the throes of economic depression.

10 Sebastian DeGrazia, *Of Time, Work, and Leisure* (1960), indicates that the suburban migration involved 50 million people. See pp. 138–139.

11 Eric Johnston, *America Unlimited* (1942), as cited in Richard Polenberg (ed.), *America at War: The Home Front, 1941–1945* (1968), p. 36.

12 *Fortune* (November 1969). This issue, dealing with "Youth in Turmoil," deals with the failing interest of American youth in questions of free enterprise, or in entering fields of business.

13 Harry Braverman, *Labor and Monopoly Capital: The Degradation of Work in the Twentieth Century* (1974). In the orthodox tradition of Marxism, Braverman deals with degradation in the productive process. While he moves in the direction of confronting the cultural implications of the "universal market," he doesn't confront the broadest social realm in his grasp of capitalist integration. Nevertheless, the book is of great importance in an understanding of the social implications of modern monopoly capital.

BIBLIOGRAPHY

Abbott, Grace. *The Child and the State.* New York, 1938.
Adams, Henry. *The Education of Henry Adams.* Boston, 1918.
Adorno, Theodor W. *Prisms.* London, 1967.
Agee, James. *Let Us Now Praise Famous Men.* 2nd ed. New York, 1966.
Allport, Floyd Henry. *Social Psychology.* Boston, 1924.
Anderson, Sherwood. *Letters.* Boston, 1953.
————. *Memoirs.* New York, 1942.
————. "Notes on Standardization." *Double Dealer.* New Orleans, 1921.
Andrews, Benjamin R. "The Home Woman as Buyer and Controller of Consumption." *Annals of the American Academy of Political and Social Science,* CXLIII (May 1929), 41–48.
Ariès, Philippe. *Centuries of Childhood.* New York, 1962.
Aronowitz, Stanley. *False Promises.* New York, 1973.

Baritz, Loren. *Servants of Power: A History of the Use of Social Science in American Industry.* Middletown, Conn., 1960.
Barthes, Roland. *Mythologies.* New York, 1972.
Barton, Bruce. *The Man Nobody Knows.* New York, 1924.
Benjamin, Walter. "The Work of Art in the Age of Mechanical Reproduction." *Illuminations.* New York, 1968.
Benson, C. E., Lucas, D. B. "The Historical Trend of Negative

Appeals in Advertising." *Journal of Applied Psychology*, XIII, No. 4 (August 1929), 346–356.

Bernays, Edward L. *Biography of an Idea: Memoirs of a Public Relations Counsel.* New York, 1965.

———. *Crystallizing Public Opinion.* New York, 1923.

———. *Propaganda.* New York, 1928.

Bernstein, Irving. *The Lean Years.* Boston, 1960.

Bloomfield, Meyer. "The New Profession of Handling Men." *Annals of the American Academy of Political and Social Science*, LXI (September 1915), 121–126.

Boone, Gladys. *The Women's Trade Union Leagues in Great Britain and the United States of America.* New York, 1942.

Boothe, Viva. "Gainfully Employed Women in the Family." *Annals of the American Academy of Political and Social Science*, CLX (March 1932), 75–85.

Borsodi, Ralph. *National Advertising Versus Prosperity, A Study of the Economic Consequences of National Advertising.* New York, 1923.

Bowlker, Mrs. ———. "The Position of Women in America." in Lapsley, Gaillard (ed.). *The America of Today.* Cambridge, 1919, pp. 229–254.

Braverman, Harry. *Labor and Monopoly Capital: The Degradation of Work in the Twentieth Century.* New York, 1974.

Brecher, Jeremy. *Strike.* San Francisco, 1972.

Bremner, Robert H. *From the Depths.* New York, 1956.

Brooks, Van Wyck. "The Culture of Industrialism." *The Seven Arts*, 1 (April 1917), 655–666.

Burtt, Harold E. and Clark, J. Camden. "Facial Expression in Advertisements." *Journal of Applied Psychology*, VII, No. 2 (June 1923), 114–126.

Butler, Elizabeth Beardsley. *Women and the Trades: Pittsburgh, 1907–1908.* New York, 1909. (Part of Kellog, Paul Underwood (ed.). *The Pittsburgh Survey.* In six volumes).

Byington, Margaret F. *Homestead: The Households of a Mill Town.* New York, 1910. (Part of *The Pittsburgh Survey*).

Calkins, Ernest Elmo. *Business the Civilizer.* Boston, 1926.

Chandler, Alfred Dupont. *Giant Enterprise, Ford, General Motors, and the Automobile Industry.* New York, 1964.

Chase, Stuart. *The Economy of Abundance.* New York, 1934.

———. *The Nemesis of American Business.* New York, 1931.

———. *The Tragedy of Waste.* New York, 1925.

———. Schlink, F. J. *Your Money's Worth.* New York, 1927.

Clark, Alice. *Working Lives of Women in the Seventeenth Century.* New York, 1968.
Cummings, E. E. *Complete Poems, 1913–1962.* New York, 1972.
Curti, Merle. "The Changing Concept of 'Human Nature' in the Literature of American Advertising." *Business History Review,* XLI, No. 4 (Winter 1967), 335–357.

Davis, Mike. "The Stop Watch and the Wooden Shoe: Scientific Management and the Industrial Workers of the World." *Radical America,* Vol. VIII, No. 6 (January-February, 1975).
DeGrazia, Sebastian. *Of Time, Work, and Leisure.* New York, 1960.
Dell, Floyd. *Love in the Machine Age, A Psychological Study of the Transition from Patriarchal Society.* New York, 1930.
Demos, John. "The American Family in Past Time." *The American Scholar,* 43, No. 3 (Summer 1974), 422–446.
Dorr, Rheta Childem. *What Eight Million Women Want.* Boston, 1910.
Draschsler, Julius. *Democracy and Assimilation.* New York, 1920.
Dreiser, Theodore. *The "Genius."* Cleveland, 1915.
Durstine, Roy S. *This Advertising Business.* New York, 1929.
Dutten, George Barton. *The Threat of Leisure.* New Haven, 1926.

Ellul, Jacques. *The Technological Society.* New York, 1967.
Ewen, Stuart. "The Capitalization of the Cosmos." (Unpublished manuscript, 1969).

Filene, Edward A. *The Consumer's Dollar.* New York, 1934.
———. "Mass Production Makes a Better World." *Atlantic Monthly* (May 1929).
———. "A Simple Code of Business Ethics." *Annals of the American Academy of Political and Social Science,* CI (May 1922), 223–228.
———. *Successful Living in the Machine Age.* New York, 1931.
———. *The Way Out: A Forecast of Coming Changes in American Business and Industry.* Garden City, N.Y., 1924.
Fitch, John A. *The Causes of Industrial Unrest.* New York, 1924.
Foner, Philip S. *History of the Labor Movement in the United States.* New York, 1947.
Fortune Magazine Editors. *The Amazing Advertising Business.* New York, 1957.
Frank, Lawrence K. "Social Change and the Family." *Annals of the American Academy of Political and Social Science,* CLX (March 1932), 94–102.

Franken, Richard B. "Advertising Appeals Selected by the Method of Direct Impression." *Journal of Applied Psychology*, VIII, No. 2 (June 1924), 232–244.

Frederick, Christine McGaffey. *Selling Mrs. Consumer.* New York, 1929.

Furniss, Edgar. *Labor Problems.* Boston, 1925.

Gale, Zona. *Friendship Village.* New York, 1910.

———. *Neighborhood Stories.* New York, 1914.

Giedion, Siegfried. *Mechanization Takes Command.* New York, 1948.

Gilbreth, Lillian. "Efficiency Methods Applied to Kitchen Design." *Architectural Record,* (March 1930), 291.

Ginsberg, Eli and Berman, Hyman. *The American Worker in the Twentieth Century: A History Through Autobiographies.* New York, 1963.

Glauberman, Naomi. "Home Sweet Home, The *Ladies' Home Journal* 1911–1926." (Unpublished manuscript, 1969).

Goode, Kenneth M. and Powel, Harford, Jr. *What About Advertising?* New York, 1927.

Goodsell, Willystine. *A History of the Family as a Social and Educational Institution.* New York, 1915.

Gordon, George. *Persuasion: The Theory and Practice of Manipulative Communication.* New York, 1971.

Gramsci, Antonio. *Selections from the Prison Notebooks.* New York, 1971.

Graves, Mrs. A. J. *Woman in America.* New York, 1841.

Groves, Ernest. *The American Family.* Chicago, 1934.

———. *The Drifting Home.* Boston, 1926.

———. Brooks, Lee M. *Readings in the Family.* Chicago, 1934.

———. Ogburn, William Fielding. *American Marriage and Family Relationships.* New York, 1928.

Gundlach, E. T. *Facts and Fetishes in Advertising.* Chicago, 1931.

Gutman, Herbert. "Work, Culture, and Society in Industrializing America." *American Historical Review,* 78, No. 3 (June 1973), 531–588.

Hartmann, George W. and Newcomb, Theodore. *Industrial Conflict: A Psychological Interpretation.* New York, 1939. (First Yearbook of the Society for the Psychological Study of Social Issues.)

Hauser, Arnold. *The Social History of Art.* Volume II. New York, 1952.

Henry, Jules. *Culture Against Man.* New York, 1965.

———. *Pathways to Madness.* New York, 1971.
———. "A Theory for an Anthropological Analysis of American Culture," in *On Sham, Vulnerability and other Forms of Self-Destruction.* New York, 1973.
Herrick, Robert. *Together.* New York, 1908.
Hess, Herbert W. "History and Present Status of the 'Truth-in-Advertising' Movement as Carried on by the Vigilance Committee of the Associated Advertising Clubs of the World." *Annals of the American Academy of Political and Social Science,* CI (May 1922), 211–220.
Hoffman, Mary E. (Under the auspices of the Ferry-Hanly Advertising Company.) *The Buying Habits of Small-Town Women.* Kansas City, 1926.
Hopkins, Claude C. *Scientific Advertising.* New York, 1923.
Horkheimer, Max. "Authoritarianism and the Family." Aushen, Ruth Wanda (ed.). *The Family: Its Functions and Destiny.* New York, 1940, 331–398.
———. *The Eclipse of Reason.* New York, 1947.
———. "The End of Reason." *Studies in Philosophy and Social Science,* 9 (1941), 366–388.
———. Adorno, Theodor. "The Culture Industry: Enlightenment as Mass Deception." *Dialectic of Enlightenment.* New York, 1973, 120–167.
———. Adorno, Theodor. *Critical Theory.* New York, 1972.
Hotchkiss, George Burton. *Advertising Copy.* New York, 1924.
Hoxie, Robert Franklin. *Scientific Management and Labor.* New York, 1921.
Hoyt, Elizabeth Ellis. *The Consumption of Wealth.* New York, 1928.
Hughes, Gwendolyn Salisbury. *Mothers In Industry: Wage-Earning by Mothers in Philadelphia.* New York, 1925.

Jastrow, Joseph. *The Betrayal of Intelligence: A Preface to Debunking.* New York, 1938.
Jones, Edgar R. *Those Were the Good Old Days: A Happy Look at American Advertising 1880–1930.* New York, 1959.
Jung, C. G. *The Undiscovered Self.* New York, 1958.

Kellor, Frances A. *Immigrants in America: Program for a Domestic Policy.* New York, c. 1915.
———. *Immigration and the Future.* New York, 1920.
———. "Neighborhood Americanization: A Discussion of the Alien

in a New Country and of the Native American in His Home Country." (Address delivered at the Colony Club, New York, February 8, 1918).

Kitson, Harry D. "Minor Studies in the Psychology of Advertising." *Journal of Applied Psychology*, V, No. 1 (March 1921), 5–13.

———. "Minor Studies in the Psychology of Advertising." *Journal of Applied Psychology*, VI, No. 1 (March 1922), 59–68.

Korman, Gerd. *Industrialization, Immigrants and Americanizers: The View From Milwaukee, 1866–1921.* Madison, Wisc., 1967.

Kyrk, Hazel. *A Theory of Consumption.* Boston, 1923.

Laird, Donald A. *What Makes People Buy.* New York, 1935.

Lee, Frederic. *The Human Machine and Industrial Efficiency.* New York, 1918.

Leiserson, William M. *Adjusting Immigrant and Industry.* New York, 1924.

Lindquist, Ruth. *The Family in the Present Social Order.* Chapel Hill, N.C., 1931.

Lucas, D. B. and Benson, C. E. *Psychology for Advertisers.* New York, 1930.

Lukàcs, Georg. *History and Class Consciousness.* Cambridge, Mass., 1971.

Lynd, Robert S. and Lynd, Helen Merrill. *Middletown: A Study in Contemporary American Culture.* New York, 1929.

Lynd, Robert S. "Family Members as Consumers." *Annals of the American Academy of Political and Social Science*, Vol. CLX, (March 1932), 86–93.

———. "The People as Consumers." *Recent Social Trends in the United States: Report of the President's* [Hoover] *Commission on Social Trends.* New York, 1933, II, 857–911.

Lyon, Leverett S. "Advertising." *The Encyclopedia of the Social Sciences.* New York, 1922, I, 475.

Marcuse, Herbert. *One-Dimensional Man.* Boston, 1964.

Marx, Karl and Engels, Frederick. *Selected Works.* (Two volumes.) Moscow, 1962.

Massachusetts Bureau of Statistics of Labor. *Report.* Boston, 1873.

Maynard, Harold, et al. *Principles of Marketing.* New York, 1927.

Mazur, Paul. *New Roads to Prosperity.* New York, 1931.

Mitchell, Broadus. *Depression Decade.* New York, 1947.

Mitchell, Robert V. "Trends in Rural Retailing in Illinois, 1926–1938." *University of Illinois Bulletin, Bureau of Business Research Bulletin Series*, No. 59 (August 11, 1939), Urbana, Ill.

Morley, Burton R. *Occupational Experience of Applicants for Work in Philadelphia.* Philadelphia, 1930.
Murray, Robert K. *Red Scare: A Study of National Hysteria, 1919–1920.* New York, 1955.
Myerson, Abraham. *The Nervous Housewife.* Boston, 1929.

Naether, Carl A. *Advertising to Women.* New York, 1928.
National Industrial Conference Board, Inc., (Harold Loeb, ed.) *Wages and Hours in American Industry.* New York, 1925.
National Survey of Potential Product Capacity. *Report.* New York, 1935.
Nevins, Allan. *Ford: The Times, The Man, The Company.* New York, 1954.
Nichols, G. H. "When Your Customers are Competitors." *Printers' Ink,* Vol. CXI (May 13, 1920), p. 20.
Nixon, Roy B. "Concentration and Absenteeism in Daily Ownership." *Journalism Quarterly* (June 22, 1945. Updated 1954).
Nourse, Edwan G. *America's Capacity to Produce.* Washington, D. C., 1934.
Nystrom, Paul H. *Economic Principles of Consumption.* New York, 1929.
———. *Economics of Fashion.* New York, 1928.

O'Dea, Mark. *A Preface to Advertising.* New York, 1937.
Ogburn, William. "The Family and Its Functions." *Recent Social Trends in the United States.* New York, 1933, II, 661–708.
Ostrander, Gilman M. *American Civilization in the First Machine Age: A Cultural History of America's First Age of Technological Revolution and "Rule by the Young."* New York, 1972.

Packard, Vance. *The Hidden Persuaders.* New York, 1957.
Park, Robert E. *The Immigrant Press and Its Control.* New York, 1922.
———. *Old World Traits Transplanted.* New York, 1921.
Pease, Otis A. *The Responsibilities of American Advertising.* New Haven, 1958.
Perrin, E. O. "The Development of Outdoor Advertising." *The J. Walter Thompson News* (February 1922).
Peterson, Theodore. *Magazines in the Twentieth Century.* Urbana, Ill., 1964.
Phelps, George Harrison. *Tomorrow's Advertisers and Their Advertising Agencies.* New York, 1929.

Poffenberger, Albert. "The Condition of Belief in Advertising." *Journal of Applied Psychology*, VII, No. 1 (March 1923), 1–9.
———. *Psychology in Advertising*. Chicago, 1925.
Polenberg, Richard (ed.). *America at War: The Home Front, 1941–1945*. Englewood Cliffs, N.J., 1968.
Pope, D. A. "The Development of National Advertising 1865–1920." Unpublished doctoral dissertation. Columbia University, N.Y., 1973.
Presbrey, Frank S. *The History and Development of Advertising*. Garden City, N.Y., 1929.
Printers' Ink: A Journal for Advertisers. Fifty Years: 1888–1938. New York, 1938.
———. *Advertising: Today, Yesterday, Tomorrow: An Omnibus of Advertising*. New York, 1963.
Prothro, James Warren. *The Dollar Decade, Business Ideas in the 1920's*. Baton Rouge, 1954.

Quinn, T. K. *Giant Business: Threat to Democracy*. New York, 1953.

Ream, Jay. "A Tip on Managing People." *Journal of Applied Psychology*, VIII, No. 3 (September 1924), 357–361.
Richardson, Anna E. "The Woman Administrator in the Modern Home." *Annals of the American Academy of Political and Social Science*, Vol. CLXIII (May 1929).
Rorty, James. *Our Master's Voice: Advertising*. New York, 1934.
Russell, Gilbert. *Nuntius: Advertising and Its Future*. New York, 1926.

Schachtel, Ernest. "On Memory and Childhood Amnesia." *Metamorphosis*. New York, 1959, pp. 279–322.
Schreiner, Olive. *Women and Labour*. Leipzig, 1911.
Scott, Walter Dill. *Increasing Human Efficiency in Business*. New York, 1917.
———. Howard, Delton T. *Influencing Men in Business: The Psychology of Argument and Suggestion*. New York, 1911.
Sheridan, Frank J. "Italian, Slavic and Hungarian Unskilled Immigrant Laborers in the United States." *Bureau of Labor Bulletin*, No. 72. Washington, D.C., September 1907.
Sklar, Martin J. "On the Proletarian Revolution and the End of Political-Economic Society." *Radical America*, III, No. 3 (May–June 1969), 1–41.
Sklar, Robert (ed.). *The Plastic Age*. New York, 1970.

Sloan, Alfred P. and Sparckes, Boyden. *Adventures of a White Collar Man.* New York, 1941.
——. *My Life With General Motors.* New York, 1960.
Speier, Hans. "Historical Development of Public Opinion." Stein-berg, Charles (ed.). *Mass Media and Communications.* New York, 1966.
Steinberg, Charles S. *Mass Media and Communications.* New York, 1966.
Stetson, Charlotte Perkins Gilman. *Women and Economics.* New York, 1900.
Stone, Katherine. "The Origins of Job Structures in the Steel Industry." *Radical America,* VII, No. 6 (November-December 1973), 19–64.
Susman, Warren I. "The Thirties," in Cobden, Stanley and Ratner, Lorman (eds.). *The Development of an American Culture.* Englewood Cliffs, N.J., 1970.

Tassin, Algernon. *The Magazine in America.* New York, 1916.
Thompson, Denys. *Voices of Civilisation: An Enquiry Into Advertising.* London, 1943.
Thompson, E. P. *The Making of the English Working Class.* New York, 1964.
——. "Time, Work-Discipline, and Industrial Capitalism." *Past and Present,* No. 38 (December 1967), 56–97.
Tipper, Harry, et al. *Advertising: Its Principles and Practice.* New York, 1921.
Trotsky, Leon. *Problems of Everyday Life.* New York, 1973.

United States Senate Document No. 62, 66th Congress. *Report and Hearings of the Subcommittee on the Judiciary.* "Brewing and Liquor Interests and German and Bolshevik Propaganda," pp. 465–472.
—— Document No. 86, 61st Congress. 2nd Session (1909–10). "Women and Children Wage Earners," I. Washington, D.C., 1910.

Veblen, Thorstein. *Absentee Ownership.* Boston, 1923.
——. *Theory of Business Enterprise.* New York, (1904, 1963).
——. *Theory of the Leisure Class.* New York, (1899, 1953).

Wallas, Graham. *The Great Society.* New York, 1919.

Walling, William English. *American Labor and American Democracy.* New York, 1926.
Ware, Norman. *The Industrial Worker, 1840–1860.* New York, 1924.
———. *The Labor Movement in the United States, 1860–1895.* New York, 1929.
———. *Labor in Modern Industrial Society.* Boston, 1935.
Watson, John B. *Behaviorism.* New York, 1924.
———. "Psychological Care of Infant and Child." New York, 1928.
Welter, Barbara. "The Cult of True Womanhood: 1820–1860." *American Quarterly,* XVIII (Summer 1966), pp. 162 ff.
Wescott, Glenway. *The Grandmothers.* New York, 1927.
Willey, Malcolm and Rice, Stuart A. *Communication Agencies and Social Life.* New York, 1933.
Williams, Whiting. *Mainsprings of Men.* New York, 1925.
———. *What's on the Worker's Mind.* New York, 1920.
Wood, James Playsted. *Magazines in the United States: Their Social and Economic Influences.* New York, 1949.
Woodward, Helen. *The Lady Persuaders.* New York, 1960.
———. *Through Many Windows.* New York, 1926.

Yoder, Dale. *Labor Attitudes in Iowa and Contiguous Territory.* Iowa City, 1929.

PERIODICALS CONSULTED:
Advertising and Selling, 1918–1930.
Forbes Magazine, 1927.
Fortune, November, 1969.
Journal of Applied Psychology, 1915–1930.
Ladies' Home Journal, 1918–1930.
Printers' Ink Weekly, 1911–1930.
Printers' Ink Monthly, 1919–1925.
System, The Magazine of Business, 1917.
Saturday Evening Post, 1918–1930.
Tri-City Labor Review, 1932.
Union Advocate and Public Forum, 1928.

INDEX

253

yia

Catalog

If you are interested in a list of fine Paperback
books, covering a wide range of subjects
and interests, send your name and address,
requesting your free catalog, to:

McGraw-Hill Paperbacks
1221 Avenue of Americas
New York, N.Y. 10020